ROUTLEDGE LIBRARY EDITIONS:
DEVELOPMENT

INTEGRATION, DEVELOPMENT AND EQUITY

INTEGRATION, DEVELOPMENT AND EQUITY

Economic Integration in West Africa

PETER ROBSON

Volume 52

Routledge
Taylor & Francis Group

LONDON AND NEW YORK

First published in 1983

This edition first published in 2011
by Routledge
2 Park Square, Milton Park, Abingdon, Oxon, OX14 4RN

Simultaneously published in the USA and Canada
by Routledge
270 Madison Avenue, New York, NY 10016

Routledge is an imprint of the Taylor & Francis Group, an informa business

© 1983 Peter Robson

British Library Cataloguing in Publication Data
A catalogue record for this book is available from the British Library

ISBN 13: 978-0-415-58414-2 (Set)
eISBN 13: 978-0-203-84035-1 (Set)
ISBN 13: 978-0-415-59572-8 (Volume 52)
eISBN 13: 978-0-203-83838-9 (Volume 52)

Publisher's Note
The publisher has gone to great lengths to ensure the quality of this reprint but
points out that some imperfections in the original copies may be apparent.

Disclaimer
The publisher has made every effort to trace copyright holders and welcomes
correspondence from those they have been unable to contact.

Integration, Development and Equity

Economic Integration in West Africa

Peter Robson
Professor of Economics
University of St Andrews

London
GEORGE ALLEN & UNWIN
Boston   Sydney

George Allen & Unwin (Publishers) Ltd,
40 Museum Street, London WC1A 1LU, UK

George Allen & Unwin (Publishers) Ltd,
Park Lane, Hemel Hempstead, Herts HP2 4TE, UK

Allen & Unwin Inc.,
9 Winchester Terrace, Winchester, Mass 01890, USA

George Allen & Unwin Australia Pty Ltd,
8 Napier Street, North Sydney, NSW 2060, Australia

First published in 1983

British Library Cataloguing in Publication Data

Robson, Peter
    Integration, development and equity.
1. Africa, West – Economic integration
I. Title
338.91'66   HC1000
ISBN 0-04-338109-X

Library of Congress Cataloging in Publication Data

Robson, Peter.
    Integration, development, and equity.
Bibliography: p.
Includes index.
1. Africa, West – Economic integration. 2. Under-
developed areas – Economic integration. I. Title.
HC1000.R62 1983   337.1'6   83-3877
ISBN 0-04-338109-X

Set in 10 on 11 Times by Preface Ltd, Salisbury, Wilts.
and printed in Great Britain
by Billing and Sons Ltd, London and Worcester.

Contents

Abbreviations

AOF	Afrique Occidentale Française (French West Africa)
BCEAO	Banque Centrale des Etats de l'Afrique de l'Ouest (Central Bank of West African States)
CEAO	Communauté Economique de l'Afrique de l'Ouest (Economic Community of West Africa)
CFA	Communauté financière africaine
ECA	UN Economic Commission for Africa
ECOWAS	Economic Community of West African States (Communauté Economique des Etats de l'Afrique de l'Ouest – CEDEAO)
FCD	Fonds Communautaire de Développement (Community Development Fund of CEAO)
FOSIDEC	Fonds de Solidarité et d'Intervention pour le Développement de la Communauté de l'Afrique de l'Ouest (Solidarity Fund of CEAO)
MRU	Mano River Union
OMVG	Organisation de Mise en Valeur du Fleuve Gambie (Gambia River Development Organisation)
OMVS	Organisation pour la Mise en Valeur du Fleuve Sénégal (Senegal River Development Organisation)
TCR	Taxe de Coopération Régional (Regional Cooperation Tax – CEAO)
UDAO	Union Douanière de l'Afrique de l'Ouest (West African Customs Union)
UDEAO	Union Douanière et Economique de l'Afrique de l'Ouest (Customs and Economic Union of West Africa)
UDEAC	Union Douanière et Economique de l'Afrique Centrale (Customs and Economic Union of Central Africa)
UMOA	Union Monétaire Ouest-Africaine (West African Monetary Union)
UNCTAD	United Nations Conference on Trade and Development
UNDP	United Nations Development Programme
UNIDO	United Nations Industrial Development Organisation
WACH	West African Clearing House (Chambre de Compensation de l'Afrique de l'Ouest)

Preface

This book analyses the issues, experience and prospects of four arrangements for economic integration in West Africa. It is intended to contribute to an understanding of their operations, and the issues that confront them, and to be of interest to students, teachers of economics and those who are professionally concerned with these arrangements.

My dormant interest in West African integration issues was re-awakened some five years ago by Oliver Knowles and I am indebted to him for his initial stimulation and advice. In the course of writing the book I have incurred a number of other debts of gratitude. I have benefited much from the encyclopaedic knowledge and perceptiveness of Eric Supper. In seeking an understanding of the issues confronting these schemes I have profited from discussions with several officials who at one time or another have been engaged in their operation. Amongst those who have been helpful I should like to mention, in particular, Dr Abubakr D. Ouattara, Executive Secretary of the Economic Community of West African States; Peter Skupsch and Paul Nambride, at one time advisers to the Communauté Economique de l'Afrique de l'Ouest, and Mrs Joy Zollner, Special Assistant to the Executive Secretary of the Mano River Union.

On the monetary problems of West African integration I have benefited from discussions with Dr Alassane D. Ouattara, Director of Research of the Banque Centrale des Etats de l'Afrique de l'Ouest, and from the very helpful advice of Sylviane and Patrick Guillaumont of the Université de Clermont. On certain issues, the perspective of the study has been influenced by advisory work that I have undertaken in connection with two of the groupings considered.

As to the manuscript itself, my principal debt is to Arthur Hazlewood, Warden of Queen Elizabeth House, Oxford, who was kind enough to read it and to provide a number of invaluable comments from his own very wide knowledge of integration issues. Parts of the manuscript were read also by Douglas Rimmer, Ranald May, Oliver Knowles and Sylviane Guillaumont, to all of whom I am most grateful for their constructive comments. The manuscript was impeccably typed by my indefatigable secretary, Mrs Helen Bremner, to whom I am particularly grateful. The map was drawn by C. B. Bremner, the University's cartographer. My wife, as usual, had the unenviable task of compiling many of the tables, and she was also kind enough to prepare the index.

I am indebted to the editor of the *Journal of Modern African Studies* for permission to use in Chapter 5 material from my article entitled 'The Mano River Union' (vol. 20, no. 4, 1982). A shorter preliminary version of parts of Chapter 4 first appeared in Ali El-Agraa (ed.), *International Economic Integration* (Basingstoke: Macmillan, 1982); I am grateful for permission to make use of it. For permission to reproduce Table 6.4 I am indebted to Bela Balassa of the World Bank. That institution has also kindly permitted the reproduction of statistical data from its *World Development Report 1982* (New York: Oxford University Press), and the *World Bank Atlas 1981* (Washington, DC: The World Bank).

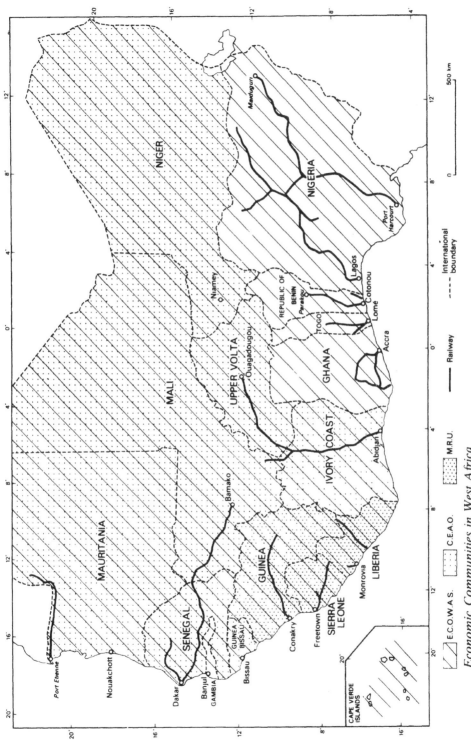

Economic Communities in West Africa

E.C.O.W.A.S. C.E.A.O. M.R.U.

—— Railway   ----- International boundary

500 km

CAPE VERDE ISLANDS

1 Introduction

Throughout the Third World, regional economic integration has been a prominent element of development strategy for more than two decades. In Africa itself, a particularly fertile ground for cooperation and integration is provided by the existence of large numbers of new states whose smallness and poverty represent severe constraints on their autonomous development. Of the forty-five states in sub-Saharan Africa, twenty-four have fewer than 5 million inhabitants. Only one – Nigeria – has a gross domestic product (GDP) greater than that of Hong Kong. Of the thirty-three countries listed in the World Bank's *World Development Report* for 1982 as 'low income', eighteen are African.

Most small poor states have limited development alternatives. Their balanced development requires larger markets, and for most of them this points to some form of regional integration. Certainly few African countries in this category – unlike Hong Kong, Taiwan, South Korea and Singapore – can expect to be able to skip the import substitution phase. Regional cooperation is thus important. It is still more so for the development of those African states that are not only poor and small, but that suffer the additional handicap of being land-locked and are consequently particularly dependent on cooperation with their coastal neighbours.

With the establishment of the Economic Community of West African States (ECOWAS) in 1975, post-colonial regional economic groupings in Africa numbered seven, of which all but one survive. Two monetary unions also exist, together with a variety of other institutions for functional economic cooperation. Since 1975, the world recession and its severe impact on Africa's economic performance have, if anything, strengthened interest in the establishment of new regional groups and the geographical extension of existing ones. Apart from the more orthodox benefits expected from them in the shape of expanded trade and investment, integration is now increasingly seen as an important element in reducing dependence and in helping to improve the bargaining position of African countries, thus contributing to their development through the broader strategy for promoting a New International Economic Order.

In April 1980 the first Organisation of African Unity (OAU) summit conference of chiefs of state to be devoted specifically to economic matters approved the Lagos Plan of Action which included the objective of creating an African common market by the year 2000, based on existing and planned regional economic communities. In December 1981, a wide-ranging agreement on trade and economic cooperation involving the establishment of a large preferential trading area in East and Southern Africa was signed by nine countries. In the same month, heads of state of the Central African countries and their neighbours, meeting in Libreville, proposed a widening of l'Union Douanière et Economique de l'Afrique Centrale (UDEAC). Another manifestation of the current concern with regional cooperation in Africa was the foundation at Lusaka in 1980 of the Southern African Development Coordination Conference (SADCC). Finally, in December 1981, Gambia and Senegal agreed to establish a Senegambian Confederation and to move towards an economic and monetary union.

A cynic might see in these recent efforts nothing more than 'a triumph of hope over experience' – as Samuel Johnson once characterised remarriage. It cannot be disputed that, during the last two decades, the record of African regional integration has not been outstandingly successful. Trade expansion has been slow and intra-group trade remains modest. Industrial coordination has often been conspicuous by its absence. Although Africa may not have reached the 'crisis' of integration that has been claimed to exist in the Third World (Vaitsos, 1978b), it has not altogether escaped the malady.

Some of the reasons for the difficulties experienced in Africa are well known. The short-run effects of integration are often not favourable: initial administrative costs are high; benefits from expanded investment and scale economies may not accrue for a long time and in any case these and other benefits are uncertain, difficult to quantify and sometimes intangible; distributional difficulties are hard to resolve where potential gains are not obvious and sure. For these reasons, although regional economic integration is certainly important as a means of loosening the developmental constraints confronting African states, it is unlikely to be an easy process. There are, nevertheless, certain pointers to a more optimistic prognosis than recent experience might appear to warrant.

In the first place, during the past two decades, much has been learned about the problems and techniques of regional integration among developing countries. In particular, the inherent limitations of orthodox customs unions and of measures for trade liberalisation are now widely recognised. It is widely appreciated that effective regional integration demands not only such measures of 'negative integration', but also what Tinbergen (1965) terms measures of 'positive integration'. These are measures designed to make an integrated market function effectively and to promote broader policy objectives. Although gaps in technical knowledge remain, if the knowledge gained from the integration experience of the past two decades is put to good use – of which there are signs – both established schemes and those in the process of formation will stand a much improved chance of making their potential contribution to development policy.

In the second place, the political context may in some respects have become more favourable. It is often suggested that in the sphere of regional integration it is not so much technical knowledge that has been lacking but the political will. During the past two decades, the emphasis of policy in most African states has been on internal political consolidation. Although these internal preoccupations have certainly not disappeared, the balance may be shifting. In part, this reflects the new importance attached to changing the international environment and to the attainment of economic objectives through political means. In part, it simply reflects a more conventional reaction to the impact of worldwide recession. Nigeria's key role in the formation of ECOWAS is an important instance of the shift in emphasis (Ojo, 1980). As a result of such changes, the hitherto missing factor in the shape of the political will to make adjustments, evolve international compromises and develop practical strategies in the cause of economic integration could conceivably prove to be less of an obstacle during the next two decades than it has been in the past.

Finally, there appears to be a renewed recognition on the part of aid agencies and donors of the role that integration is capable of playing, and of the need to provide support for regional projects, policies and perhaps institutions, including the much-needed development of transport links if that potential is to be realised. This could result in regional integration projects – frequently the Cinderellas of aid programmes – being given a much higher priority, so reducing their short-term costs and increasing benefits.

It is against this complex background that the following study examines the initiatives, experience, progress and prospects of regional integration arrangements in Western Africa. Despite their interest and potential importance, these have not hitherto received the attention accorded to similar initiatives in other parts of Africa or in other parts of the Third World.

The outline of the study is as follows. Chapter 2 indicates the limitations of the orthodox analysis of customs unions in the context of developing economies and sketches the outlines of an alternative approach that provides the conceptual framework for the subsequent empirical appraisals. Chapter 3 discusses practical strategy and policy issues of integration initiatives involving developing countries that are neglected by orthodox analysis. Particular attention is given to the problem of determining the scope for integration, to distributional issues and to the role of transnational corporations in regional integration.

Chapter 4, the first of four chapters that discuss specific arrangements for economic integration in West Africa (the Cape Verde–Guinea–Bissau Free Trade Area is not considered), looks at the operations of the Communauté Economique de l'Afrique de l'Ouest (CEAO). The CEAO, whose establishment was decided on in 1970, represents the third attempt of the states that came into being as a result of the collapse in 1959 of the French West African Federation (with the exception of Guinea) to maintain and develop important economic ingredients of that earlier relationship. The countries initially involved were Benin, Ivory Coast, Niger, Upper Volta (four of the five members of the Council of the Entente), together with Mali, Mauretania and Senegal (the three members of the Organisation for the Development of the Senegal River – (OMVS). Influenced by Nigeria, Togo, a former French Trust Territory and the fifth member of the Entente, did not seek to join. Benin, which had initially signed the Treaty, was persuaded by Nigeria to withdraw in 1973, but, like Togo, it enjoys observer status. CEAO is an important functioning example of economic integration in Africa, and the specific ways in which it has attempted to deal with a variety of policy issues are of wide interest. More specifically, since the CEAO countries are now part of the broader ECOWAS grouping, their experience on policy issues that are only broadly outlined in the Treaty of Lagos may suggest valuable guidelines for the development of ECOWAS itself.

Chapter 5 discusses the formation and progress of the Mano River Union (MRU). This group was inaugurated in 1973 and initially comprised Liberia and Sierra Leone. The two countries had been involved in 1964, together with Guinea and Ivory Coast, in an earlier attempt to establish a West African free trade area, but this initiative fell victim to political conflict between Ivory Coast and Guinea. Towards the end of the 1970s, Guinea, already moving in a number of ways towards a less isolationist stance, initiated discussions with a view to membership of MRU, and in 1980 it formally acceded. So far, the economic achievements of the group have been modest, but the institutional framework for cooperation between the two founder members has been established.

The most ambitious grouping of all is the Economic Community of West African States (ECOWAS), which was inaugurated in 1975.

This sixteen-country grouping includes all states of the West African sub-region, which together constitute a geographical zone larger than Western Europe. The member states of MRU, CEAO and Senegambia are also part of this wider grouping. ECOWAS includes some of the richest and most populous countries in Africa, several of which possess immense mineral resources. It also includes most of the poorest countries in Africa – and indeed a large proportion of those in the whole world. Nowhere else have attempts been made to integrate so many diverse countries, and the potential problems involved are immense. Chapter 6 outlines the Treaty of Lagos, which underpins ECOWAS, and reviews the progress so far made in implementing it. Particular attention is given to the present pattern of trade among its members, and to the possible implications of trade liberalisation. Evidence of recent research studies is brought to bear on the discussion of the prospective gains from integration.

Chapter 7 discusses the economic implications of the agreement on a Senegambian confederation, which was concluded in December 1981, following an abortive coup in The Gambia earlier in the year and Senegalese intervention. The Confederation Agreement provides for the development of an economic and monetary union between the two countries.

Chapter 8 discusses monetary and payments aspects of economic integration, the implications of monetary integration, the operations of the West African Monetary Union and of the West African Clearing House.

The concluding chapter summarises the central policy issues confronting economic groupings of developing countries and briefly comments, from these points of view, on each of the four West African schemes reviewed in the book.

2 Towards a Developmental Theory of Integration among Developing Countries

What are the benefits that developing countries can expect to derive from participation in regional economic groupings?

Orthodox comparative static analysis based on the customs union theory of Byé (1950) and Viner (1950) attributes such gains to increased production arising from specialisation according to static comparative advantage, that is, essentially to static resource allocation gains. The orthodox theory analyses the effects of integration principally in terms of the *trade creation* and *trade diversion* that would result. Trade creation refers to a shift from the consumption of higher-cost domestic products in favour of the lower-cost products of other member states. This reduces the cost of goods previously produced domestically. Trade diversion refers to a shift in the source of imports from lower-cost sources outside the regional bloc to a higher-cost source within it. The merits of integration are then evaluated using the relative magnitudes of trade creation and trade diversion as the sole criterion. A union that is on balance trade creating is regarded as beneficial, whereas a trade-diverting union is regarded as detrimental.

This analysis has only a limited bearing on the evaluation of gains from integration in developing countries. A major reason for this is that its standpoint is that of free trade, so that any gains derive solely from a move towards free trade involving, on balance, the reduction or elimination of inefficient or high-cost domestic industries. If this were the objective of integration, and the sole source of gain from it, even greater gains could be obtained by reducing tariffs on a non-discriminatory basis, or by removing protection for domestic enterprises altogether, and by importing domestic requirements of the products of displaced industries from outside at world market prices (Robson, 1980), although this proposition has been questioned (Wonnacott, 1981).

The neoclassical analysis of integration among developing countries starts from an entirely different developmental standpoint. It is assumed that there is a valid case for protecting certain activities in developing countries – particularly industry – either for the purpose of increasing income or the rate of growth, or in order to attain certain non-economic objectives that are sought for their own sake. To attain the latter may entail economic sacrifice, but that would not negate the argument.

The implications of economic integration in these terms can best be considered within a broader framework than that often employed, in which account is formally taken of (1) economies of scale; and (2) divergences between private and social costs of production. The gains from integration can then be analysed in the particularly relevant context of opportunities to exploit economies of scale that cannot be secured in single national markets, and the implications of market imperfections can also be brought out. Imperfections typically arise when certain goods and services do not fully pass through the market, thus giving rise to external economies and diseconomies, or when government policies distort the prices of factors and goods.

The following analysis adheres to the original formulation of developmental theories of integration in its explicit recognition of industrialisation and the structural transformation of economies as development objectives. This entails that the gains from integration must be exploited on a mutual basis, by the exchange of markets within a customs union or common market or other preferential area, so that they can be secured without a sacrifice of the structural developmental objectives of individual member states.

THE COMPARATIVE STATICS OF INTEGRATION WITH SCALE ECONOMIES

Figure 2.1 depicts demand and cost conditions in the domestic markets of two countries – H, the home country, and P, the partner country – that are contemplating the establishment of a customs union for a product produced by existing industries or for a planned new product. D_H is the home country's demand curve for the product, and AC_H is the average cost curve. D_P and AC_P are the corresponding demand and cost curves in the prospective partner country. D_{H+P} represents the combined customs union demand curve. P_W represents the constant price at which the product can be imported from W, the rest of the world. Terms of trade effects are thus ruled out.

It is assumed that there is a single producer in each country enjoying internal economies of scale, so that the traditional assumption of perfect competition that is so much at variance with the situation found in developing countries is not maintained. The introduction of

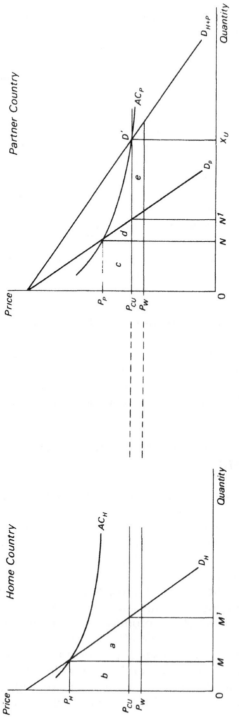

Figure 2.1 *A Customs Union with Economies of Scale*

economies of scale in this way, however, gives rise to certain problems of monopolistic behaviour (Robson, 1980, ch. 3), which are not crucial to the analysis. To avoid these, it is assumed that tariffs are 'made to measure' at levels designed to make the tariff-inclusive import price equal to average costs, including normal profits, and that in each country the domestic price is determined by the cost of imports from the rest of the world, plus the tariff.

Prior to the formation of a customs union, the home country produces and consumes OM, which amount sells domestically at a price OP_H. A tariff of P_wP_H is required to make the industry viable. The more efficient partner country produces and consumes an amount ON at price OP_P with a lower tariff P_wP_P. If the two countries integrate, and production is undertaken by the producer whose cost conditions are more favourable – which may not necessarily occur (Robson, 1980, ch. 3) – the combined requirement of the market, OX_U, would be produced by the partner country at a price OP_{CU}, the required union tariff being P_wP_{CU}. Consumption in the home country increases to OM^1 and in the partner country to ON^1.

In this case, country H would gain an amount equal to the areas $b+a$. These are the traditional gains from trade creation, although now to be seen in the context of scale economies. Country P would gain c from the cost reduction effect (Corden, 1972) plus d, representing the gain in consumers' surplus, plus e, representing the gain from sales to the partner country at prices in excess of world market prices. Up to this point, except for the introduction of scale economies, this analysis appears to be as defective as the orthodox analysis in terms of its inability to provide a rationale for integration – at least for country H. For country H there is no merit in this outcome as compared with the alternative of free trade, since it could obtain similar benefits from a non-discriminatory unilateral tariff reduction to P_wP_{CU}. However, there is a difference in this case for country P, since it could not secure as large gains for itself in the absence of a customs union merely by unilaterally reducing its tariff to the same level. As the figure clearly indicates, its gains exceed any losses incurred by the home country, whose industry would disappear with the advent of customs union.

Under such circumstances, if a range of industrial production exists in both countries, of which these demand and cost curves merely illustrate one case, it may be possible, depending on the empirical relationships, for both countries to gain by exchanging markets in a customs union. In this way, for instance, H could provide the requirements of the combined market for some other product for which it is the lowest-cost producer in the prospective union. The outcome then would be that all could gain potentially by the exchange of markets. This is essentially the approach to the analysis of integration among developing countries that was first set out by Cooper and Massell (1965) and was subsequently elaborated by Dosser (1972), modified here to incorporate scale economies. There may be problems in the exchange of markets which is crucial to this approach, if some of the members of the integration grouping are not the least-cost producers within the union of any, or of a sufficient range of, products, so that their developmental and industrialisation objectives could not necessarily be attained within a simple customs union. This raises issues of regional policy that are discussed elsewhere.

It is clear that, in the conditions assumed, the expanded union industry remains a high-cost producer by comparison with the rest of the world, even allowing for the utilisation of economies of scale. This means that the case for integration in these terms must rest on a prior case for protection. This might be founded either on non-economic considerations or on dynamic economic arguments, which are not encompassed in this purely comparative static analysis. For instance, to the extent that the range of important infant industry considerations comes into play, the cost curves of the relevant industries may shift downwards over time, until ultimately they become competitive. Protection may also affect the rate of growth through its impact on the rate of domestic capital formation, or – in terms of a still broader framework – through its impact on the inflow of foreign capital. These important dynamic economic arguments for protection are admirably analysed in a policy context by Corden (1974).

THE IMPACT OF DOMESTIC DISTORTIONS

The static analysis itself can be brought closer to the conditions relevant to developing economies by introducing domestic distortions that are widespread in developing economies and can affect both consumption and production. A most important distortion derives from a market price of labour that typically exceeds the equilibrium rate on account of trade union activity or government minimum wage legislation. It will be assumed that domestic distortions of various kinds cause the average cost curve expressed in terms of social, that is, opportunity, costs to lie below the average cost curve expressed in terms of the actual market prices of factors of production.

Figure 2.2 presents the same basic information as Figure 2.1, but with the addition of the relevant social opportunity cost curves AC_{H1} and AC_{p1}. It is assumed that the social cost curve of country H lies throughout above the import price from the rest of the world,

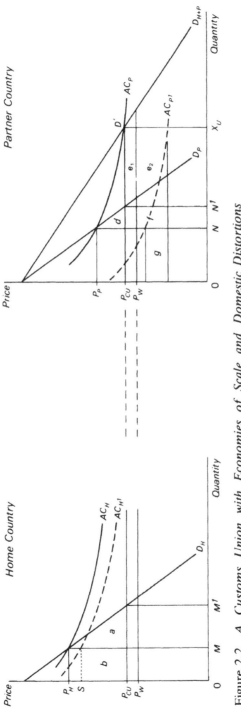

Figure 2.2 A Customs Union with Economies of Scale and Domestic Distortions

whereas for country P it lies below the import price for certain ranges of output. Prior to integration, social costs in H exceed the world market price so that, in static terms, negative social profits are earned: opportunity costs exceed the price of imports. The rationale for government support for this industry must then be based either on dynamic gains or on non-economic objectives – if it is not based on misconceptions!

Following integration by the formation of a customs union, there are, as in the previous case, orthodox gains from trade creation for the home country. Its consumption gain will be a as before, but the production gain is smaller, being denoted by the lower part of b that falls below the horizontal dotted line at S.

The gains to the partner country can in this case be decomposed into the following elements:

(1) the consumption gain, d as before;
(2) the cost savings arising from expanded output with scale economies, but now computed in terms of social costs by reference to the original level of output (g);
(3) the gains from sales to the partner country. These are now equal to the larger area $e_1 + e_2$, of which the first component, as before, represents an income transfer by H to country P, while the latter, equal to the sales to the partner times the difference between the world market price and domestic social costs, represents the net social gain made possible by market unification;
(4) the social benefits derived from the additional production for the partner's home market. These are measured by the additional amount consumed as a result of the fall in price multiplied by the difference between the world market price and the domestic social cost of the additional output (f).

More generally, it would be necessary to distinguish at least three cases according to whether (1) both, (2) neither, or (3) only one of the countries is able to produce with positive social benefits before integration. In the first case, the country losing industry will incur social losses. In the second case, production is socially unprofitable throughout the union in static terms, because social costs exceed social returns as indicated by world market price. Protection for this industry prior to integration could then only be justified on dynamic (infant industry, etc.) grounds, or on non-economic grounds. Of course, integration would permit the country whose industry expands to move down its cost curve and so to cut its losses or even to achieve social gains, whether or not the level of post-union output is socially profitable. But, in the event of an agreement providing for compensation in terms of the excess cost of union imports of a type discussed in the following chapter, it would be possible for the country that expands its industry to reap gains only if the level of output were socially profitable after allowing for compensation. The country whose industry shuts down would, in the second case, gain from a reduction of social losses. The third case is intermediate. Before integration, the home country protects and produces inefficiently in social terms. The partner country whose industry is to expand protects, but in social terms operates efficiently. This is the case assumed in Figure 2.2.

If an industry can become socially profitable at higher levels of output, this appears to raise the question, in terms of this model, why it needs a protected regional market. The answer to this lies partly in factors outside this simple model, such as transport costs (the import and export price here being assumed to be identical) (Wonnacott, 1981).

If, however, the relevant case is one in which neither country is able to produce with positive static social benefits before or after integration, then, just as for the similar situation in which distortions are absent, it will be mutually advantageous for the two countries to integrate and combine their markets so that each remaining industry produces at a larger scale for the combined market and at a lower cost than under autarkical policies only if either (1) there are non-economic considerations underlying industrialisation policy, or (2) the dynamic considerations excluded from this comparative static analysis are evaluated as of sufficient importance to offset the excess static costs.

SOME LIMITATIONS AND IMPLICATIONS

The essentially static and neoclassical analysis that has been presented in this chapter rests on a number of highly restrictive assumptions. In a fuller theoretical treatment it would be desirable to develop the analysis in several directions. It would be of interest first to adapt the analysis to the empirically important situation of fragmented production where several firms produce at scales of output lower than the minimum level of average costs. The analysis of a competitive situation in which, exceptionally, a falling long-run supply curve was generated by technological external economies might also merit consideration. A further useful extension within a strictly neoclassical formulation would be to incorporate the implications of international capital flows, as has been done by Tironi (1982) from a purely distributional point of view. A still more important extension would be to analyse the effects of integration on growth through its impact on capital formation and to attempt to incorporate the all-important dynamic considerations (Corden, 1974). There are of course also many important political and social considerations, which, though highly relevant to a broad appraisal of integration issues, can find no place in any neoclassical analysis however broadened (Vaitsos, 1980) and which indeed cannot easily be embodied in any formal analysis. Despite its exclusion of these aspects, the simple analysis presented in this chapter appears to capture many of the essential issues and it provides a necessary basic conceptual foundation for analysing contemporary integration initiatives among developing countries.

The framework can of course be used both to evaluate the gains that integration and trade liberalisation may afford with respect to an already existing, fragmented industrial base, or to throw light on the prospective developmental gains from rationalising emergent structures of production and new investment, in the context of a regional industrial policy. In practice, however, the amount of trade expansion that follows trade liberalisation and integration among developing countries is often extremely limited, in the short run, principally because pre-integration levels of industrial development in the member countries are low. Expansion from a very low base frequently encounters supply bottlenecks, especially of skills. A lack of opportunity for immediate trade expansion is clearly not an adequate guide to the merits of integration, because the gains from rationalising the emergent structures of production may in due course be very considerable. It is indeed self-evident that, the more underdeveloped economies are at the time of their integration, the less important will be the gains from rationalising the existing structure of production relative to those to be derived from rationalising new industrial production.

One important implication of the broader conceptual framework outlined in this chapter is that the neoclassical static concepts of trade diversion and trade creation lose much of their relevance as criteria for the evaluation of integration initiatives for two main reasons: (1) trade expansion may be a source of gain for the exporting country no matter whether, in nominal terms, trade creation or trade diversion underly it; (2) trade creation in itself may be detrimental for an importing country. A policy of economic integration for a group of developing countries may thus be warranted even if the conditions for 'nominal' static trade creation do not exist, so long as there are sufficient gains to be anticipated from the prospective rationalisation of new production or, indeed, from the rationalisation of investment in the regional infrastructure.

Nevertheless, there is no automatic case for economic integration amongst a purely random group of developing countries. A case needs to be evaluated on its merits for any proposed group. Its strength will depend partly though not exclusively on the empirical significance of the following factors: the weight attached to industrialisation in their development policy; the possibilities, if any, of exporting manufactures to world markets rather than to protected regional markets; the magnitude of scale economies, in particular in prospective regional industries; the differences in the cost of producing industrial products in the different member countries; the geographical location of markets in member countries; the costs of transporting raw materials and finished products within the region.

The varying importance of these factors in different developing countries makes it highly unlikely that each and every developing country could benefit from regional integration. An optimal development strategy for some countries would undoubtedly entail first supplying their domestic markets by relatively low-cost, 'first-stage' import substitution, involving the production of consumer goods, followed by a direct move into export for world markets, without at any stage seeking the support of regional integration arrangements. In the conditions of the later twentieth century, relatively few less developed countries (LDCs) appear to enjoy such prospects. For many of them (particularly those in Africa that suffer the constraints of minuscule domestic markets and that are land-locked), trade and economic integration on a regional basis are likely to represent an indispensable prior stage for making a transition to higher levels of development and a more open economy. The merits of regional integration as a desirable development strategy for a large number of African countries in the conditions of the 1980s are not negated by the impressive but possibly exceptional experiences of South Korea, Taiwan, Singapore, Hong Kong and other newly industrialising countries.

In the foregoing analysis it has been emphasised that regional integration finds its principal economic justification in certain gains – dynamic in particular – which accrue from protection. There are of course a number of entirely separate arguments for integration. One of these is based on the opportunity it may provide for increasing the member countries' bargaining power in external economic relations if they bargain as a group, rather than individually. This argument has long been recognised and in practice it appears to have been not unimportant in motivating the formation of regional groups – notably of ECOWAS.

The formation of groupings has in practice also been motivated by a desire to reduce external dependence in a variety of important spheres. It is questionable whether the character of development that has actually been stimulated by regional groupings has had this effect – indeed, quite the contrary outcome may have been produced (Vaitsos, 1978a). But to a considerable extent this must be attributed not so much to the inappropriateness of regional integration as a strategy for achieving a reduction in dependence as to the unwillingness of the members of LDC groupings to harmonise their non-tariff policies. The failure to cooperate in other policy areas has had many repercussions, not least for the impact of integration on foreign investment inflows.

3 Practical Strategy and Policy Issues of Integration among Developing Countries

The effects and the policy issues of economic integration are much the same for groupings of advanced and developing countries, but the economic contexts are very different. The particular structural features of developing countries combine to produce a situation in which certain aspects of policy, though also relevant in advanced countries, assume a dominant importance in developing countries. In broad terms, the principal difference is that in advanced market economies the market can be largely left to take care of the integration process. As Wiles once put it, admittedly before there was any experience of the Byzantine possibilities of the EEC, 'it [the market] integrates quietly and impersonally, while prime ministers are in bed' (Wiles, 1968). The difference can be exaggerated, but it is without doubt important, and it dictates a different integration strategy in developing groupings from what might be appropriate in advanced market economies. Specifically, it points to a need for a more positive integration strategy, in the Tinbergian sense.

The principal policy issues confronting integration initiatives involving developing countries are in fact concerned with matters to which the orthodox theory gives little or no attention, its theoretical foundations largely ruling them out of consideration. The three principal issues are:

(1) the determination of the appropriate scope and direction of regional trade, development and specialisation in operational terms;
(2) the issue of equity in the distribution of benefits;
(3) policy towards foreign investment and multinational or transnational corporations.

COMPARATIVE ADVANTAGE, REGIONAL SPECIALISATION AND INVESTMENT

The first issue, to ascertain the desirable extent and direction of industrial development and the character of regional specialisation, is basic. It requires effectively an appreciation in operational terms of the comparative advantages of the community as a whole and of particular countries within it. When money costs do not reflect social opportunity costs because of unemployment, infant industry considerations, external economies and diseconomies, economies of scale, foreign exchange shortages and, in particular, fiscally induced price or cost distortions, the price system will not provide a guide. Desirable patterns of trade and development will have to be directly evaluated.

The problem of ascertaining the operational scope for regional specialisation and development when distortions are severe and widespread arises both for trade liberalisation in the context of the already existing industrial structures of member countries, and for new investment opportunities created by the unified market. For major new industrial investments at community level involving community enterprises (joint ventures), there will often be no adequate substitute for a full social cost–benefit analysis using established techniques, at any rate if such enterprises seek, or are to be accorded, special privileges not available to all new investment. Similarly, a social cost–benefit analysis will be required of the new infrastructure investment in roads, ports and railways for which a unified market will create a need, both to facilitate trade liberalisation and to facilitate new investment. Such investment, particularly in transport and communications, will often be a precondition of exploiting the gains from economic integration. In Africa this is particularly so. Despite important advances in the past two decades, infrastructure facilities are underdeveloped and are, moreover, still largely geared to the exportation of primary products to Europe rather than to intra-regional trade, which, partly for this reason, is often physically difficult, time-consuming and relatively costly. To overcome these kinds of constraints upon regional integration, regional infrastructure projects may be indispensable if a unified market is to be made a reality – for example, the Mano River bridge between Liberia and Sierra Leone, which reduced the distance between the two capitals from over 1,000 km to 550 km. Fortunately, well-justified regionally based infrastructure projects are particularly favoured by aid donors.

Although social cost–benefit analysis has a vital role for evaluating certain major new investments, and community joint ventures, it clearly cannot be employed for determining the comparative advantages of whole economies and of their existing industrial sectors. For this purpose – of vital importance in terms of imparting a proper direction to integration policy – alternative approaches must be devised.

During the past two decades, estimates of effective protection coefficients and of domestic resource cost coefficients have been widely used for general trade policy evaluations. There are certain problems concerning the significance of these methods, of which it is important that policy-makers should be aware (Findlay, 1971; Little and Mirrlees, 1974). But no better practical method has yet been devised for making broad policy evaluations in relation to protection and trade policy on an economy-wide basis. An extension of the method to illuminate issues of regional economic integration is overdue.

In essence, the method assumes that the combined effects of tariffs, quantitative restrictions and other protective measures on a domestic producer's output and inputs can be represented by the effective protection coefficient (EPC). This coefficient expresses the impact of protection on domestic value-added in production. Specifically, it is defined as the ratio that domestic value-added after applying protective measures bears to value-added expressed at world market prices. (The latter amount corresponds to the domestic currency equivalent of the net foreign exchange saved through import substitution or earned through the exportation of the products of the protected industry.) An EPC greater than 1 means that, at the existing exchange rate, protective measures provide positive incentives to the firm or activity. An EPC of less than 1 indicates that, on balance, protective measures discriminate against the firm or activity. A negative EPC would signify that the firm or activity produces a loss of foreign exchange to the national economy.

In calculating the EPC, domestic value-added is expressed in terms of actual domestic market prices. If calculation stops short at this point, it will overestimate the resource cost of production to the national economy for two main reasons: (1) if above-normal profits are being earned, or (2) if, because of unemployment, market wages exceed shadow wages. If domestic value-added is corrected for these points in an attempt to arrive at the social opportunity cost of the activity, and the corrected amount is then compared, as before, with the value-added at world market prices, a coefficient is arrived at that is termed the domestic resource cost of foreign exchange (DRC). The DRC represents the value of domestic resources expended in saving a unit of foreign exchange by import substitution, or earning a unit of foreign exchange by export activity, expressed as a proportion of the actual exchange rate.

DRC coefficients can be used to provide a ranking of activities in terms of comparative advantage. A coefficient of less than 1 indicates that the activity is socially profitable. A coefficient of more than 1 indicates that the activity is socially unprofitable. A negative coefficient would signify that the activity actually results in a loss of foreign exchange. DRC coefficients require correction if the exchange rate is overvalued. This would not affect the ranking of activities according to comparative advantage and domestic resource cost but would be relevant to any decisions about the merits of expanding, contracting or discontinuing different industries. Coefficients of DRC corrected for the value of foreign exchange are sometimes termed coefficients of real costs of production.

The use of this approach for policy purposes in regional groupings is subject to important limitations. The purely statistical limitations must first be borne in mind. The calculations normally relate to one year only and are affected by the degree of capital utilisation. The estimates of capital stock may be subject to substantial error as may estimates, for instance, of the equilibrium price of foreign exchange. The quality of the statistical data in the different countries will also vary and may result in bias.

Statistical problems apart, although calculations of this kind may be useful for giving direction to integration policies in the short and medium run, it must be borne in mind that they are derived from historical data relating to industries set up primarily to serve national markets alone, and at different times. Their technologies may not be the most up to date, or the most appropriate to serve a unified market in which scale economies can be more fully exploited. Essentially they provide a snapshot of the position at a point in time when a moving picture would be more useful for eliciting trends and directions. They should therefore be interpreted in the light of information on the structural changes in progress in the different member countries. Examples of these evaluations and a further discussion of their limitations will be found in Chapters 4 and 6.

POLICIES FOR EQUITY AND BALANCE

The second crucial policy issue that confronts regional groupings of developing countries is to design measures to produce an equitable inter-state distribution of the benefits of integration. Until a relatively advanced level of economic development is attained, domestic manufacturing industries in developing countries normally require a significant level of protection if production is to be commercially viable, even when tariff-free access to a regional market is assured. If this protection is provided principally by tariffs or by other 'second best' price-raising devices, as is normally the case, difficulties over the regional distribution of the costs and benefits of integration, which in any event are likely to arise, will be greatly exacerbated.

The direct costs of import substitution, which are represented by the excess private cost of domestic production over the cost of imports from the outside world, will be borne by community members in proportion to their consumption of import substitutes. On the other hand, the benefits of import substitution (which may include an enhanced rate of return to capital and labour, expanded employment and wage incomes, a more balanced economic structure, savings in foreign exchange and an increased rate of economic growth) will accrue primarily to those countries in which the new productive capacity is located.

In these circumstances, if the protected activity justified by regional integration does not spread itself over the regional market so that each country attracts an equitable share, conflicts of interest are bound to be perceived. The experience of countries and regional groupings in which the distribution of industry is left to the working of market forces suggests that such a regional balance is unlikely. On the contrary, a marked 'polarisation' of development has tended to occur, disproportionately favouring regions and states with relatively high *per capita* incomes or relatively large domestic markets. Typical examples of this phenomenon are the concentrations of industry, commerce and services found in and around Abidjan and Dakar in the CEAO, in Nairobi in the defunct East African Community, and in Guatemala City and San Salvador in the Central American Common Market. Polarisation is reflected in marked imbalances in intra-regional trade in manufactures. Corrective mechanisms are essential to deal with this problem if economic integration is to be durable.

If the interests of inter-state equity are to be served as well as those of economic efficiency, corrective policies will have to be employed to promote equitable and balanced development in a regional grouping and appropriate instruments devised for this purpose. The choice lies between (1) income transfers, and (2) instruments to effect a change in the emergent patterns of trade and development, which income transfers do not do. Under (2) there is a choice between methods that principally rely on the market and methods that rely on deliberate, planned rationalisation of industrial development. In each case the objective is to bring about profitable specialisation subject to the requirements of balanced development. The difference is that in the first case the emphasis is on the attainment of the objective through the operation of market forces by the negotiation of a suitable, generally applicable structure of fiscal and other incentives, which is expected to work broadly in the desired directions. With the other approach the emphasis is first on determining the appropriate scope for specialisation in new industries and then on utilising administrative controls to implement the desired changes in the pattern of production.

Fiscal Compensation

Fiscal compensation by intergovernmental income transfer through the budget is one possible mechanism. It is an element in the financial arrangements that underpin UDEAC, the Southern African Customs Union (SACU), CEAO and ECOWAS. Earlier uses of this mechanism are reviewed in Robson (1971).

A commonly advocated criterion for compensation is the net *tariff* revenue forgone as a result of buying the products of other member states. The merits and demerits of this criterion can best be appreciated by briefly considering the principal factors that would influence the distribution of costs and benefits in an economic grouping of developing countries. Benefits as well as costs must be considered since the magnitude and distribution of the former will determine the 'additional' resource and fiscal base from which member states could finance any required compensation payments.

In the short run, given the existing structure of industry, the costs of integration would be mainly dependent on the excess cost of importing from member states products that might otherwise be imported from the rest of the world. The benefits to the exporting member state, in the absence of excess capacity, would be derived from its opportunity to sell to partner countries on more favourable terms than to other countries – yielding higher prices, earnings and tax revenues. Where, as is often the case, excess capacity exists in the exporting country, so that larger outputs would be involved in trade expansion, these benefits will be much greater, and will include expanded production and employment and the additional incomes so generated.

In the longer run, the benefits will also depend on the integration-induced level of industrial activity and the terms on which resulting community trade is conducted, but the location of new industrial activities and operations will itself be affected by the preference afforded by the regional market. As to the long-run cost to importing countries, this will be greater than the impact cost to the extent that, for some products, preferences or free trade giving rise to importation from a partner state would imply a loss of opportunity in the importing country to establish certain industries that could otherwise be viable under protection, and that could be capable of generating income, employment and public revenues and of contributing to a diversification of the country's economic structure. Indeed, such losses can also arise in the short run when existing industries are displaced by imports from a partner – for example, as a result of trade creation.

Both in the short and the long run, the distribution of costs and benefits will be reflected in the induced intra-group trade of each member with its partners, and in the induced trade balance of each member of the group with the rest of the group. A concern with intra-group balances is therefore justifiable, although it must be emphasised that *recorded* trade balances and *induced* trade balances are unlikely to be identical.

The rationale for compensation for revenue losses must be viewed in the light of the considerations that have just been outlined. The object of compensation is *not* to provide compensation for revenue losses *per se*. This is merely a convenient criterion. The rationale is that in certain circumstances such losses correspond to higher import outlays and therefore to the static loss of national income suffered by an importing country from its extension of a preference to member countries. Likewise, in certain circumstances, the preference measures the lowest value that attaches to the benefit that the exporting country receives in terms of national income from its opportunity to export to a partner on preferential terms, and may thus serve also as a basis for determining compensation contributions.

Fiscal compensation, whether based on 'revenue' losses or some other indicator, should facilitate trade liberalisation by reducing or removing one of its major potential costs for the less advanced countries, but it is for several reasons an unsatisfactory approach. In the first place, from the free trade point of view, a country that is simply compensated for its customs revenue losses (that is, for the cost of trade diversion) would not necessarily be better off in a customs union than it would be if it pursued a non-discriminatory tariff policy. Secondly, from the alternative, and more relevant, standpoint of the objectives of a protectionist policy, this measure disregards the benefits of development that a country forgoes, notably in the shape of increased value-added and employment in manufacturing, when it imports from its partners instead of producing import substitutes for itself, where that option exists. In other words, even that part of trade expansion that involves trade creation – actual in the case of existing industries, potential in the case of those planned – may involve a cost. A country that loses existing industries as a result of trade liberalisation may thus suffer a loss of real income for which there is no counterpart in tariff revenue losses. (There may be direct tax losses as taxable income falls, however.) These considerations justify the refusal of the more recently established regional economic groupings to rely solely on fiscal compensation to deal with the problem of the distribution of benefits. Where compensation is provided – as it is in UDEAC, CEAO, ECOWAS and SACU – it is one element in a package of policies designed to alter the distribution of benefits in part by influencing the regional distribution of industry. The measures potentially available for this purpose operate either indirectly through the provision of market incentives, or directly through the adoption of industrial specialisation agreements having administrative or legislative sanction.

Fiscal Incentives to Influence the Emergent Location of Industry

Fiscal mechanisms may be used to influence the location of new enterprises in an economic grouping, either with, or without, the support of inter-country fiscal transfers. In the first case, fiscal compensation may be linked to the promotion of productive investment in less favoured member countries through the provision of supplementary fiscal investment incentives financed by the community. Alternatively, compensation funds may be used to finance the provision of loan finance on a subsidised basis for investment in industry or in infrastructure through the medium of regional development banks, as was done by the Central American Bank for Economic Integration and the East African Development Bank, as happens, to a limited extent, in the Entente countries and CEAO, and as is envisaged in the ECOWAS Fund.

Even if inter-country fiscal transfers are not utilised for these purposes, either because they are not made, or because they are not earmarked but take the form of a straight interbudgetary transfer, a harmonisation of national fiscal incentives can still be employed as a means of influencing the distribution of industrial activity. By this means, less developed member countries may be authorised to provide more generous investment incentives (from their own budgetary resources), while the agreement excludes a counterproductive bidding up of incentives by more advanced members. Several economic groupings of LDCs have formulated measures of incentive harmonisation with these considerations in mind and, at the limited level of regional policy, the European Economic Community operates such a policy. All of the West African groupings envisage a harmonisation of incentives, but it is not yet clear whether this will result in agreed differentials to serve the interests of regional policy.

Remedies for regional imbalances may also be sought through the limited retention of intra-group tariffs. In newly formed groupings, less developed member countries could be permitted to adopt a slower pace towards full trade liberalisation than their more advanced partners, as was the practice in the Andean Pact arrangements, and as is envisaged in ECOWAS – though only modestly. Indeed, the indefinite retention of moderate intra-group duties by less developed members may even be justifiable in certain circumstances, since that procedure might be less costly to the group (Cooper and Massell, 1965) in producing a desired regional balance than would a simple customs union.

Regional Industrial Policy and Planned Industrial Specialisation

The alternative to relying on fiscal harmonisation in conjunction with the forces of the market to influence the emergent pattern of industrial development is to attempt to shape developments positively by adopting an agreed regional industrial policy that involves some planned specialisation for new industrial development, whether that takes place in the private sector or alternatively on the basis of joint ventures operated by the member states themselves. The adoption of regional industrial policies and industrial harmonisation is increasingly given greater weight in evolving regional integration initiatives.

The history of earlier arrangements is one of difficulties of both negotiation and implementation. There are many reasons for this record, including uncertainty as to the outcome, different evaluations of the costs and benefits involved on the part of different participants, and different concepts of equity. These will not disappear. There are, however, two other reasons that often handicapped earlier attempts, which are partly remediable.

The first remediable factor is bound up with negotiating procedures. Often the agreed location for each new industry has been the subject of separate negotiation. This is a relatively uncomplicated procedure. Negotiations can be undertaken as projects come forward, and do not have to be held back until a portfolio of well-developed project studies is built up. Nevertheless, this approach has the defect that it does not necessarily provide an immediate benefit for each participant from each new development. Governments have been understandably reluctant to agree to the establishment of industries in partner countries, partly to serve their own markets, when by so doing they impose tangible and immediate costs upon themselves in the shape of real income losses (reflected in revenue losses), in return for a prospect of uncertain benefits at some future time when some other project in its turn is assigned to them. One way of dealing with this problem is to prepare an indicative regional programme for a specific range of industrial projects. Member countries could then be invited to endorse such a programme, the projects in which would be allocated within the region in such a way that each country received an acceptable share. This approach has the practical advantage of providing an incentive for each participant to agree on each programme. Its practicability would, however, require the simultaneous availability of several well-worked-out projects. If the procedure is not to hold back economic development, it will demand a considerable and sustained planning effort on the part of the community's institutions, and close cooperation with the planning agencies of the member countries.

Planning Models

A number of attempts have been made to bridge the gap between theory and the needs of the policy-maker by the development of planning models designed for evaluating regional industrial programmes of this kind. This approach underlies the industrial strategy of the Cartagena Pact countries, and of the Association of South-East Asian Nations (ASEAN). It merits close attention by policy-makers in LDC regional groupings.

The projects in such programmes for industrial cooperation typically concern investments that are relatively large in relation to the total size of the developing economies in question, and for some of them there may be substantial economies of scale. It is therefore desirable, on general grounds, to approach the problem of programming for regional economic cooperation in general equilibrium terms, since large-scale projects will have effects not only on the suppliers and customers, but also on other industries.

Such an approach for the analysis of the effects of capacity expansions in a limited number of projects with economies of scale was first worked out for a single country by Westphal (1971). He sets such investment projects in a general equilibrium framework by considering not only the industry in which the project is to be inserted, but also the rest of the economy by adding the input–output relations for the entire economy and specifying those between it and the projects under investigation.

Westphal's model has subsequently been extended by Mennes (1973) to allow for a number of countries and various possible locations, and in this form it becomes directly relevant to regional integration. Mennes' model is a typical programming one (for the most part linear), but allowance is made for economies of scale in one part of his study. This extension necessitates the use of mixed integer programming methods. Optimality is defined in terms of minimising cost of production.

Although such general equilibrium approaches to the analysis of integration among less developed countries are in principle highly desirable, their operational application confronts two important limitations: (1) to apply them, one needs input–output tables for each country; and (2) it is not possible to solve the model except for, say, two or three projects for possible division among two or three countries. Operational programming involving a considerable number of projects and several countries can at best make use of a partial equilibrium method.

This less demanding mode of evaluation was first applied to regional integration in a study that dealt with the assignment of investment projects among Latin American Free Trade Area (LAFTA) countries (Carnoy 1972). The study employs a modified linear programming model to find the cheapest way of supplying the projected demand for the products in question, balancing the economies of scale made possible by the expansion of production at a single point against the accompanying increase in transport costs. The welfare gains (defined as resources saved) as a result of importing from the minimum-cost location as compared with importing from the USA or producing nationally are also computed. The costs to the region in terms of increased production cost of producing goods at various suboptimal locations (that is, those requiring outlays higher than the minimum costs of production and transportation) are also determined.

To be able to apply even this less demanding approach, it is necessary to estimate the extent of the markets for the products and input requirements at all relevant scales of output, together with the transport costs of inputs and outputs both within and outside the region. Lack of data on any of these would hinder its use. In practice, failures of information are likely to be acute in the estimation of output demands and, in particular, of input requirements. Although it may be possible in a general way to ascertain what inputs a project uses, and in approximately what quantities, it is extremely difficult *ex ante* to estimate how these requirements would vary for any industry, from one country to another. This was a major weakness of the study for ASEAN that utilised this approach (UN Economic Commission for Asia and the Far East, 1973), but it is a general limitation of all studies of this kind.

Investment planning models can form an important ingredient of an evaluation of regional industrial programmes, but evaluation cannot be confined to the essentially neoclassical mould that underlies them. From the standpoint of individual participating countries, at any rate, an evaluation of a regional programme cannot usefully depend only, or even chiefly, upon differences in unit process costs of production under different locational alternatives. In the first place there will be income changes associated with the change in the level of industrial activity in the region, which push the production frontier outward. In the second place there will be benefits or losses associated with changes in the structure of the economies, with particular reference to the level and character of employment, its degree of specialisation and diversification and its stability characteristics. These changes may be sought for their own sakes or because they are regarded as important elements of a policy for imparting a dynamic for development to the economy.

A second remediable reason for the lack of success with attempts at planned industrial specialisation is that although a particular regional allocation of industries may be negotiable at governmental level, that alone does not ensure the implementation of the projects in the largely market economies that characterise less developed groupings. Agreed specialisation usually implies the allocation of industries to country locations that investors regard as suboptimal. Investment that is excluded by means of licensing or some other device from the privately preferred country location may not be undertaken anywhere else in the region, unless the perceived disadvantages are offset. Past attempts to operate industrial cooperation agreements among developing countries have sometimes given insufficient weight to this consideration.

The resolution of this second aspect of the implementation problem requires measures to ensure that the envisaged investment will be commercially profitable, either by the provision of adequate fiscal incentives or by other means. Of current African integration groupings, the Mano River Union is the only one to envisage this approach and to make specific provision for dealing with this problem.

TRANSNATIONAL ENTERPRISES AND REGIONAL INTEGRATION

The third policy issue or set of policy issues confronting integration groupings of developing countries has to do with three important problems that are neglected by the orthodox theory of customs unions and economic integration. These concern foreign direct investment, monopolistic practices and access to technology. With negligible exceptions (Kemp, 1969; Scully and Yu, 1974), the orthodox theory completely disregards all three by assuming that technology is constant, that competition is perfect and that capital is immobile internationally. In developing countries and in integration groupings amongst those countries, the issues that arise when these conditions are not satisfied have a common focus in the activities of multinational or transnational corporations (TNCs), whose activities have assumed a dominant role in nearly all present-day regional groupings. The implications of the operations of TNCs for the theory and practice of integration therefore need careful consideration.

Does the orthodox analysis explaining the structure of intra-group trade and the gains from intra-group trade continue to be relevant in the face of the major role assumed by TNCs in virtually all regional economic groupings among developing countries? Without question, the operations of TNCs may affect in important ways the possibilities of improved resource allocation in a regional grouping, and may also have an important bearing on the ability of member countries to attain other policy objectives such as reduced dependence, closer inter-industry linkages, enhanced external bargaining power and an equitable share of the benefits of integration. On one view indeed (Vaitsos, 1978a), the relationship between integration and the operation of TNCs is so close that the policies of the group and of individual members towards them are the primary issue in contemporary integration processes.

Three principal aspects merit discussion in the context of integration: (1) the relationship between the operations of transnational corporations and improved resource allocation (static and dynamic efficiency); (2) the character of integration promoted by TNCs and its relationship to the diverse policy objectives that underly integration initiatives; and (3) the impact of TNCs on the distribution of the gains from integration, both amongst the partner countries themselves and between the partner countries on the one hand and the foreign enterprises on the other. An evaluation of the issues that arise in these areas and of empirical evidence inevitably prompts the question of whether harmonised policies towards TNCs are required in regional groupings.

Transnational Corporations and Economic Efficiency

The potential impact of TNCs on static resource allocation and on dynamic efficiency in regional groupings is clearly bound up with their repercussions at large in these respects. During the past two decades there has been much discussion of this issue (Johnson, 1970; Behrman, 1972; Dunning, 1981), in the course of which emphasis has been given to the benign role of TNCs in facilitating a transfer of technology, in part through their ability to 'internalise' the process, thus avoiding important market costs. Only recently has there been much consideration of the specific significance of TNCs in the context of regional integration (Vaitsos, 1978a; Mytelka, 1979; Langdon and Mytelka, 1979; Tironi, 1982) and the possible qualifications required thereby to the orthodox view of integration. In these discussions, the behaviour of TNCs is often viewed as harmful.

If the view taken of the operation of TNCs is that their primary objective is to achieve least-cost production in their operations, it would follow from the resource allocation standpoint that no qualification to orthodox integration theory would be called for by their operations in the context of regional groupings.

An alternative view of TNCs, more consistent with modern theories of the firm and available evidence, explains their conduct and performance in terms of two alternative objectives, namely, the maximisation of their long-run profit, and the maintenance of an acceptable share of the market. These alternative strategies may imply an intra-regional impact on intra-regional imports and exports and on the intra-country distribution of benefits, which would not be predicted by orthodox integration theory.

One important way in which, on this more realistic view, the conduct and policies of TNCs may affect resource allocation is through their territorial allocation arrangements, which are forms of restrictive business practices. These arrangements may extend to provisions determining which parts of the enterprise will export what products and to where, and which parts of the enterprise will import products from where; the levels of production and the types of activities that can be undertaken by a subsidiary, including the degree of processing to be undertaken and the degree of forward or backward integration; the kinds of capital equipment and inputs used; the use of trade marks and technology. The operation of any of these factors could partly offset, or in extreme cases might completely nullify, any hoped-for effect of trade liberalisation on intra-group trade.

Pricing policy, which is closely linked with territorial allocation, is a second aspect of TNC policy with important implications for regional integration. Of particular importance are the transfer prices used in intra-firm transactions. These may be significant both for the distribution of the benefits of integration and for the potential resource allocation gains. Manipulation of transfer prices can be used to transfer profits outside the region and within it, either in order to minimise tax liabilities or to influence exports or imports. At this point, it is the trade impact that is the question: if a subsidiary is required to buy essential inputs at a price higher than would be charged by a third-party supplier, it is less able to export.

It is true that if the TNC should be the sole producer of a particular product in the region, the quantities of goods traded and the direction of trade and specialisation need not be affected by the phenomenon of transfer pricing (Horst, 1973). More generally, however, the manipulation of transfer prices of final products to cross-subsidise a subsidiary in order to eliminate local competitors, to maintain a position of market dominance, or to hinder potential competitors from entering the market, as appears to occur (UN Conference on Trade and Development, 1978), must affect not only trade patterns but also the character of industrial production within the group and the intra-regional distribution of benefits.

The actual impact of TNCs on resource allocation within a regional grouping through such policies will ultimately depend on how they perceive their interests to be affected by integration schemes.

The Interests of TNCs in Integration

On *a priori* grounds a TNC might be expected to be anxious to promote integration where national markets are small and it is not itself already involved in other member countries through parallel direct investments. This was the situation in the Central American Common Market prior to integration, and also in several of the smaller African groupings, though this is less often true as development proceeds. In groupings of medium- or larger-sized developing countries by contrast, the attitudes of TNCs towards the effective integration of production might *a priori* be expected to be less favourable, since any one enterprise is more likely to be simultaneously involved in other member countries. Even if it is not itself involved, it may face competition from competing multinational corporations in those countries. Rationalisation of TNC activities throughout the region through market integration may then not be in the interests of any one TNC. Even where TNCs favour integration within a grouping of developing countries, it is likely to be only for final products. With respect to inputs, it is often in the commercial interest of a TNC to promote increased production and input links with parent firms outside the region, rather than with enterprises in other member countries, so that the task of developing intra-industry linkages in the region may be rendered still more difficult when the integration process relies heavily on TNCs. In the same way, the typically high dependence of TNCs on often highly specialised imported inputs maintains, and may enhance, the degree of external economic dependence of the member countries and the influence of TNCs in the group. In these ways, paradoxically, some of the broader objectives of economic integration and development policy may be frustrated unless vigorous countervailing policies can be implemented.

The operation of these factors cannot be expected to have any simple, uniform effect on static or dynamic efficiency in regional groupings. The outcome will depend on the character of the economies integrating, on the exact nature of the governmental industrialisation policies pursued and, above all, on the extent to which non-tariff policies are harmonised within the group. But where the member states compete vigorously amongst themselves for foreign investment by investment incentives, and a regional industrial development policy is lacking, it cannot be expected that the operations of TNCs will result in optimal resource allocation within the region.

Nevertheless, it is important to recognise that any adverse effects on resource allocation accompanying the behaviour of a transnational may largely result not from conduct specific to transnational corporations, but from the conduct of *any* profit-maximising enterprise that possesses market power and that operates by reference to market signals that distort the framework of market integration. This is the relevant point to make about the fragmentation of TNC production that is often found in LDC groupings, with a replication of production facilities (Langdon and Mytelka, 1979; Chapter 4 below). To the extent that this is so, the remedy lies in the adoption of a regional industrial policy and a related fiscal incentives policy for *all* enterprises rather than one specifically directed towards transnationals, and in the adoption of more rational pricing systems throughout the region so that self-interest and community interest are harmonised. This is not to deny that transnationals normally possess greater bargaining power than purely regional enterprises, so that even if a common policy should be established their global base will often enable them to control elements of business strategy that a purely regional enterprise could not.

In the end, although integration may give TNCs additional scope for promoting efficient resource allocation, experience suggests that it is also likely to result in an increase in the market power of the TNCs. As a result, both resource allocation and the distribution of the benefits of integration may be affected by their operation, and not necessarily favourably. Harmonised codes of investment, fiscal concessions, enterprise behaviour and possibly ownership may consequently be important if integration is to serve the policy objectives of the member states. Where TNCs have a major role, as they do in most developing countries, further reasons thus exist for supposing that market integration and trade liberalisation are an insufficient economic strategy for promoting improved resource allocation, an equitable distribution of benefits and other developmental objectives.

CONCLUSION

This chapter has discussed the issues in three crucial policy areas confronting integration groupings of developing countries, namely, the scope for comparative advantage and the direction of industrial development, which raises basic issues of development strategy; the problem of balanced development and of inter-state equity in the distribution of costs and benefits arising from integration; and, finally, the issue of policy towards multinational or transnational corporations.

Economic analysis provides no cut and dried guidance in these areas. The policies are concerned with issues on which there is not and cannot be full knowledge, and where subjective considerations, uncertainty and bargaining strategies inevitably assume key roles. Nevertheless, it is possible and useful to evaluate relevant provisions and behaviour in relation to these areas in an illuminating way. Thus, although the concept of equity is not an objective one, the likely impact of integration arrangements can be revealingly assessed by reference to a base line that insulates members from net costs as compared with a situation of non-participation. The distribution of benefits above this base line can then be enumerated for evaluation.

In the four following chapters the structure, operation and achievements of four West African integration initiatives are discussed and assessed in the light of the principal policy issues that specifically confront them.

4 a Communauté Economique de l'Afrique de l'Ouest

INTRODUCTION

The Economic Community of West Africa (Communauté Economique de l'Afrique de l'Ouest — CEAO) represents the third attempt
of the majority of the states created out of the former federation of
Afrique Occidentale Française (AOF) to maintain and improve
established arrangements for regional economic cooperation. The
two earlier initiatives, resulting in the successive establishment of the
West African Customs Union (UDAO) in 1959 and of the Customs
Union of West African States (UDEAO) in 1966, both failed. The
reasons for their failure are numerous and complex, and some are
now mainly of historical interest. Technical, administrative, political
and economic factors all played a part. Amongst the economic, a natural
desire on the part of newly independent states to be free to utilise
their principal instrument of fiscal policy, namely the tariff, in the
interests of national development was not unimportant. The principal
reason for failure undoubtedly lay in the inherent defectiveness of an
orthodox customs union as an effectual policy instrument for African
regional cooperation. It is true that certain necessary improvements
had been made in UDEAO, notably in an acceptance of the necessity
of intra-regional tariff protection in a bloc that lacked a regional
policy, and in the establishment of a permanent machinery of
administration that had previously been lacking. But in its almost
exclusive concern with trade liberalisation UDEAO remained, like
its predecessor, an expression of an approach to integration that Tinbergen (1965) has designated as 'negative'. It was hardly at all concerned with measures of 'positive integration' that are indispensable
if a combined market area is to function effectively in terms of
resource allocation objectives and to promote other broader joint
policy objectives, in particular the important distributive objectives.
These limitations were to play a large part in the ineffectiveness, in its
turn, of UDEAO that had become apparent by 1969. Its members
were nevertheless persuaded to make a further effort to place their

economic cooperation on a firmer basis. Their new initiative took the form of proposals for a much more ambitious arrangement for regional integration that went well beyond the removal of trade barriers and the formation of a customs union to include positive measures to promote regional economic cooperation and development on an equitable and balanced basis. The agreed provisions are embodied in the Treaty of Abidjan (CEAO, 1973), which came into effect in 1973 on its ratification by Ivory Coast, Senegal, Mali, Mauretania, Niger and Upper Volta.

Although CEAO undoubtedly expresses important shared economic interests on the part of its founder members, its formation equally certainly was precipitated by politically motivated manoeuvres, partly French inspired. These were directed towards offsetting Nigeria's growing influence in the region and, more specifically, at countering her own attempts to organise a pan-West African economic community of anglophone and francophone states. In February 1971, in the course of his first African tour, President Pompidou had gone out of his way to exhort the francophone countries 'to harmonise their efforts so as to counterbalance the heavy weight of Nigeria'. Later that year, Presidents Senghor and Houphouët-Boigny of Senegal and Ivory Coast composed long-standing differences and by affirming their own commitment to CEAO virtually assured its formation. Nevertheless, several of the smaller francophone countries remained hesitant about the wisdom of participating once again in an exclusively francophone economic grouping. The trading and other interests of Niger, Togo and Benin clearly pointed to the unwisdom of their too close association with a trading bloc of which Nigeria was not a member. For its part, Upper Volta felt misgivings about joining a group that would exclude Ghana. For its own reasons, which are discussed in Chapter 6, Nigeria made vigorous attempts to exploit these reservations and to head off the establishment of CEAO. It was in the end successful in detaching Benin, which, having previously been courted actively by Nigeria through financial and other inducements, was eventually persuaded not to join CEAO, although initially it had been a signatory of the draft pact. Togo too was persuaded to remain aloof from the CEAO initiative. Its position however had from the outset differed from that of the other prospective members since, as a former French Trust Territory, it had never formed part of AOF. Nor did it become a member of the subsequently established customs unions, preferring instead to maintain a stance of non-discrimination in trade. In 1972 Togo entered the other camp when its head of state, President Eyadema, together with General Gowon of Nigeria, agreed to establish the nucleus of a new West African grouping for economic cooperation that would embody both anglophone and francophone countries. This agreement was the springboard for the later foundation of ECOWAS.

Nigeria's insistent claim that CEAO was not an adequate basis for regional cooperation, although evidently motivated in part by self-interest, was not wholly groundless. CEAO is certainly too small to exercise any considerable bargaining power in the international sphere, and its combined domestic market is far too small to permit low-cost production in a large number of industrial activities. Nevertheless, its members had much experience of cooperation amongst themselves. Moreover, the national implications of a narrower grouping such as CEAO could be more readily assessed by its prospective members than could those of a much wider polyglot grouping. For these reasons alone, it would be surprising if the possibilities for real and immediate, if ultimately more limited, economic cooperation were not perceived to be greater for the smaller, francophone grouping than for the much broader scheme urged by Nigeria. Although the establishment of CEAO was without doubt encouraged by external political influence, it does not follow that it is incapable of generating significant economic benefits to its members.

THE ECONOMIES OF THE MEMBER STATES

As a background to the operations of the Economic Community of West Africa it is convenient to review briefly the present economic conditions and recent development of its member states. (Detailed statistics on the structure of production and growth and on the structure of trade, growth and export in the CEAO are included in Tables 6.2 and 6.3 on pp. 90 and 91.) In general terms, the Community's most striking characteristics are its vast land area, small populations and generally low incomes (see Table 4.1). In 1980, the combined population of the Community amounted to a mere 34 million, and this was spread over an area larger than Western Europe and roughly half the size of the USA. Population distribution is very uneven, for much of the vast area is predominantly Sahelian in character and, being of low or negligible agricultural productivity, is very thinly populated. In those areas, crop production is at present confined largely to riverain flood plains such as those of the Niger and Senegal rivers.

The aggregate GNP of the Community in 1980 amounted to some $17,150m. (World Bank, 1982), of which the Ivory Coast alone accounted for more than half. Average income *per capita* amounted to $510. All member states fall into the World Bank's low-income category except for Ivory Coast, whose *per capita* income of $1,150 –

Table 4.1 *Population, Income and Growth*

Country	Population (m) 1980	Area ('000 sq. km)	Population density (inhabitants per sq. km)	Rate of population growth 1970–80	Aggregate ($m.)	GNP (1980) % of total Community	Per capita ($) 1980	GNP per capita (real av. annual growth percent) 1960–80	Real GDP growth (average annual growth percent) 1960–70	Real GDP growth (average annual growth percent) 1970–80
Ivory Coast	8.3	322	25.8	5.0	9,550	56	1,150	2.5	8.0	6.7[a]
Upper Volta	6.1	274	22.3	1.8	1,280	7	210	0.1	3.0	3.5
Mali	7.0	1,240	5.6	2.7	1,340	8	190	1.4	3.3	4.9
Mauretania	1.5	1,031	1.6	2.5	660[b]	4	440[b]	1.6[b]	..	1.7
Niger	5.3	1,267	4.2	2.8	1,760	10	330	−1.6	2.9	2.7
Senegal	5.7	196	29.1	2.8	2,560	15	450	−0.3	2.5	2.5[a]
Community	33.9	4,330			17,150		510			

[a] 1970–79.
[b] The estimates of GNP and growth rate for Mauretania should be treated with reserve. Alternative World Bank estimates (e.g. *Atlas*) suggest a substantially lower GNP ($530m., and a negative annual growth rate (−0.7%)).
.. not available.
Source: World Bank (1982b), Annex, *World Development Indicators*.

higher than in any other African country south of the Sahara except South Africa – places it squarely into the middle-income group.

The pattern of economic growth experienced by the Community's members during the past two decades is diverse. Exceptionally high rates of growth of real GDP were experienced by Ivory Coast for the whole of the period 1960–80, but the growth rates of the other members were much lower. Rates of growth of *per capita* real GNP, reflecting the impact of both population growth and of profit and interest remittances abroad, were lower and, at best, hardly more than modest, reaching 2.5 per cent only in Ivory Coast. In fact, negative real *per capita* annual growth rates are recorded for Niger (−1.6 per cent) and Senegal (−0.3 per cent).

Twenty years ago, at the beginning of the 1960s, all six countries were fairly typical low-income primary producing economies, and the principal domestic determinant of their economic activity was the production of primary products for export. This was reflected in the generally high share of agriculture in the GNP for all countries except Senegal, where industrial and service activities had been developed in Dakar on a scale disproportionate to Senegal's own domestic requirements in order to serve the needs of the whole of AOF.

Agricultural production in the Community is mainly carried on by traditional agriculturists, partly for subsistence but partly for the market. Modernised plantation and estate agriculture is also found, in particular in Ivory Coast (where its operation has underpinned the substantial growth and diversification of agricultural production in recent years), to a limited extent in Mali (in rice and groundnuts), and in Upper Volta (sugar). Cash crops are mainly produced for export, but some, for example cotton and, to a limited extent, rubber and certain food crops, are important ingredients of local consumption and manufacture. The most important cash crops are cotton, coffee, cocoa, groundnuts, sugar cane, rice, rubber and pineapples.

Most members are highly specialised on one or two of these: Senegal – groundnuts, Mali – cotton and groundnuts, Upper Volta – cotton, Niger – groundnuts and cotton. At the beginning of the period, Ivory Coast's agricultural production was also highly specialised, and three-quarters of its export earnings were produced by coffee and cocoa. By 1975, although these two crops continued to be important (accounting in that year for nearly a half of export earnings), others such as cotton, rice, sugar, pineapples and rubber had become significant.

Livestock rearing, often with a nomadic base, is of major importance in several countries, including Mali, Upper Volta, Mauretania and Niger. Other important natural products include timber in Ivory Coast and fish in Mauretania.

Even today, the domestic economic performance of the CEAO countries is heavily dependent on agriculture and livestock production. The unsatisfactory growth record of certain Sahelian member states is principally attributable to the severe impact of the droughts of the early 1970s upon agriculture and livestock. But during the past two decades, important structural changes have occurred in two of the Sahelian member states and in Ivory Coast, so that it is no longer only Senegal whose economic performance is significantly influenced by activity in other productive sectors.

In the Sahelian countries of Niger and Mauretania, the source of the changes has been mineral development, which has largely mitigated the disastrous impact of drought on their incomes. Throughout the whole of the period 1960–80, Mauretania enjoyed a substantial income from the production and export of iron ore. In 1980, income from this source, which accounted for more than 25 per cent of GNP and 75 per cent of export earnings, exceeded that generated by agriculture and animal husbandry. Niger's mining sector is of more recent origin, but it too has similarly provided the principal recent dynamic element of that country's growth. In Niger, income generated by mining has not yet overtaken agriculture's contribution to GNP but growing income from uranium production has nevertheless underpinned a fairly quick recovery from the effects of drought, and has supported growth in other sectors.

The other member state whose economic performance has become significantly dependent on developments outside agriculture is Ivory Coast, where the change results not from mineral development, but from success in creating a varied modern manufacturing sector. In 1980, income generated in Ivory Coast's manufacturing sector surpassed that of agriculture in its contribution to GNP, despite the considerable absolute expansion in agricultural production that had been achieved over the previous twenty years. The rapid development of Ivory Coast's manufacturing industry that has occurred during the past two decades was based initially on the managed substitution of domestic products in its home market for goods previously imported from Senegal. This was supported by bilateral trade deals with Senegal and by the development of exports to other countries of the Community, notably Upper Volta and Mali. Export markets were also successfully created outside CEAO in the rest of the West African region. In this wider, intra-regional trade, Ivory Coast has now succeeded in becoming West Africa's leading exporter, far outstripping Nigeria and Ghana in importance. Ivory Coast's substantial industrial growth is due not merely to its natural advantages in the shape of a substantial domestic market, access to a labour force and relatively low energy costs, but also to the provision of generous industrial incentives. These have been a major contributory factor in enabling Ivory Coast to overtake Senegal's initially dominant position in several major industrial sectors and to establish very strong positions in others.

An inevitable consequence of Ivory Coast's rapid industrial growth has been that, for much of the period, industrial development in Senegal has been much less dynamic, reflecting the adjustment imposed by increased competition from Ivory Coast's industries in the latter's own domestic market, in Senegal itself and in other countries of the group. Nevertheless, Senegal's industrial sector continues to generate a relatively large share of GNP (comparable to that of agriculture), and during the past decade its manufacturing sector generated a larger share of its GNP (in terms of valuation based on domestic market prices) than that of any other member of the group.

In the land-locked states of the Community and in Mauretania, some expansion of the industrial sectors has occurred from very modest beginnings, but the relative importance of these sectors, apart from mining, is much smaller than in Ivory Coast and Senegal.

The industrial structure that has grown up in the Community is typical of its income levels and size of market. In terms of a broad product classification, the most important industrial group, measured in plant numbers, is the food, drink and tobacco industry, which in 1975 numbered eighty-eight plants. (This is an unsatisfactory indicator of relative importance, but regular censuses of manufacturing are not available for all member states. These statistics of plant numbers are derived from a Community enumeration for 1975.) The chemical industry – a heterogeneous group that includes both traditional products such as paints and matches and others such as plastics that are based on newer technologies – was in second place with fifty-two units. In third place came the textile industry, which numbered thirty-two units. Industries linked to construction and building, which are effectively protected by the high costs of transporting the finished products, are also important (twenty-five units). The same consideration partly accounts for the importance of industries assembling transport goods such as coaches, autocycles and bicycles. Mechanical and electrical industries on the other hand were relatively little developed, and most of the plants in this category are small units of an artisanal character, typically involved in repair work.

Industries established in the Community fall into four distinct categories: (1) industries processing agricultural products for export (such as cotton ginning and groundnut processing); (2) industries subjecting certain imported products to a limited degree of additional processing; (3) industries producing, with mainly local ingredients, relatively simple import substitutes such as cement, bricks, textiles and beverages by means of simple technologies; (4) industries, of a processing or assembly kind, involving more sophisticated products and techniques. Ivory Coast and Senegal both possess all four types, but the industrial sectors of the land-locked countries and of Mauretania are mainly limited to the processing of primary products and minerals for export and to the production of simple import substitutes.

Of the 336 enterprises recorded in the 1975 enumeration, 139 were located in the Ivory Coast (most having been established after 1960) and a further 102 were located in Senegal. In terms of shares of combined output value, Ivory Coast accounted for some three-fifths and Senegal for one-quarter, with Niger, Mali and Upper Volta each accounting for some 5 per cent. Within each country, industrial development is highly concentrated on one or two development poles that afford infrastructure, a suitable labour force and concentrated markets.

A notable aspect of the industrial development of all the CEAO countries is its heavy dependence upon investment by European and American transnational corporations. In the industrial sectors of all member states except Mali, where the public sector is more important, and to a lesser extent in Upper Volta, the larger industrial enterprises are generally affiliates of foreign corporations that own the bulk of their capital. In textiles, for instance, except in Mali, most of the large and medium enterprises in CEAO are affiliated to foreign corporations that own between 60 and 100 per cent of the capital. Some of these transnational corporations operate in only a single member state of the Community, where they may be in competition with others, but more often they do business in more than one member state, as does the important locally based Blohorn group. The process of distribution is also undertaken by foreign-owned enterprises such as the Compagnie Française de l'Afrique Occidentale (CFAO), which operates in more than one country of the Community. In each country, moreover, a mere handful of enterprises accounts for a large part of industrial sales. Table 4.2 brings out the importance of a small number of enterprises and the dominant role of foreign ownership in their operations.

Transnational manufacturing corporations that operate in more than one country of the Community include: CFAO and its country affiliates such as the Compagnie Française de la Côte d'Ivoire (CFCI), Bata, in the footwear industry, which has establishments in Ivory Coast, Senegal and Upper Volta; Peugeot, which produces cycles, motorised cycles, tyres and inner-tubes in Ivory Coast and Upper Volta; Air Liquide, which has establishments in all six states; Carnand, a producer of metal cans and boxes, which has affiliates in

Table 4.2   *CEAO: Share of Sales and Distribution of Ownership of Larger Foreign Enterprises, 1975*

Country	No. of enterprises	% of industrial sales	Share of foreign ownership ( ) = French-owned share
Ivory Coast	10	43	63 (40)
Niger	5	80	57 (25)
Senegal	10	59	75 (70)
Upper Volta	5	65	44 (35)

Source: Abstracted from Banque Ouest-Africaine de Développement (1978), p. 155.

Ivory Coast and Senegal; Wonder, which produces batteries in Ivory Coast, Upper Volta and Mali; Nestlé, which, as Capral, produces instant coffee in Ivory Coast and also operates in Senegal. In food products, Grands Moulins de Paris operates in Ivory Coast and Upper Volta, and in beverages, Brasserie et Glacière d'Indochine operates in Ivory Coast, Senegal, Upper Volta and Niger. In the textile industry, a complex system of interlocking financial participations has been created both within and between countries through which transnationals such as Gonfreville, Texunion, Riegel (USA), Schaeffer, Rhone Poulenc (Textiles) and CFAO participate in a variety of combinations in developments in Ivory Coast, Senegal, Niger and Upper Volta. The dominant importance of multinational corporations in the Community and their interlocking activities probably influence the structure of trade, specialisation and industrial development of the region as much, if not more, than the partial integration of product markets that is brought about by the actions of the national governments operating through Community instruments such as the regional cooperation tax. To that extent, their activities will also influence the intra-regional distribution of the costs of cooperation and the distribution of costs and benefits between the states. of the region on the one hand and foreign investors on the other.

THE PROVISIONS OF THE TREATY OF ABIDJAN

The Community's objectives as expressed in the Treaty clearly imply a more positive approach to economic cooperation than that of its predecessors. In its statement of aims, emphasis is placed on the promotion of a harmonised and balanced economic development of the member states. The instruments for achieving this general objective are to be active policies of cooperation and integration in a variety of policy areas including steps to develop trade in agricultural and industrial production on an organised basis.

The foundation of the Community is nevertheless the creation of a unified regional market. The principal instruments for bringing this about are: (1) the establishment of a common external tariff (CET) within twelve years; (2) the introduction of free trade in products of local origin (such as livestock, agricultural products, fish and mineral products) that have not undergone industrial processing (*produits du cru*); and (3) the institution in approved cases of a special preferential import duty regime, termed the regional cooperation tax (Taxe de Coopération Régionale – TCR) for traded manufactured products that originate in member states. This involves the substitution of a single duty (the TCR) at an effectively lower rate in substitution for all import duties that would otherwise be levied. The level of the TCR is fixed on a product by product basis by the Council of Ministers. Internal indirect taxes imposed without discrimination on both imports and domestic products may be levied additionally. Orthodox customs union arrangements for the circulation of transferred imports, and the reimbursement of corresponding duties, are specified in Protocol I (CEAO, 1973) and in a subsequent ministerial decision 12/77/CM (*Journal Officiel*, 1977).

A novel feature of the Treaty is its provision for the payment of compensation to offset the revenue loss (*moins-value budgétaire*) arising from the importation of products that are subject to the TCR to the extent of two-thirds of the assessed loss. Compensation is effected through the Community Development Fund (Fonds Communautaire de Développement – FCD). The FCD derives its resources from contributions from member states, which in total are equivalent to the aggregate assessed revenue loss. Each member's contribution to the FCD is determined by its relative share of the global value of intra-CEAO exports of manufactures for the year in question. The difference (equivalent to one-third of the assessed revenue losses) between the receipts of the FCD and its compensatory payments is made available to support projects of Community interest in the member states.

Apart from its orthodox trade and customs aspects, the Treaty also contains more novel ones of great potential importance relating to the development of common Community policies in other fields. These concern notably the preparation according to a stated timetable of a draft programme of industrialisation, a draft statute for multinational corporations, and proposals for harmonising fiscal incentives for investment. Joint policies and measures are also envisaged in other sectors of economic activity, including scientific and technological research, energy production and distribution, the development of industry and mining, the development of tourism, meat production, and the coordination and development of transport and communications, although in none of these areas is a timetable specified for implementation. The policy content of these provisions is likewise unspecified. To implement and develop common policies, the Treaty established Community Offices for Agricultural Development, Industrial Development, Trade Promotion, Livestock and Meat, and Fisheries. Other significant provisions of the Treaty relate to the free circulation of persons and capital and the right of Community nationals to establish enterprises and to practise their professions without discrimination.

Unlike the situation in some other regional groupings, it was unnecessary for the Treaty to concern itself with monetary and payments issues since all of its signatories except Mali and Mauretania participate (together with Benin and Togo) in a common central bank (Banque Centrale des Etats de l'Afrique de l'Ouest – BCEAO) and share a common currency (the CFA franc), which is pegged to the French franc and is freely convertible. The Malian franc is also freely interchangeable with the CFA franc at a fixed parity.

To operate the Community, provision is made for the establishment of four main Community institutions in addition to the FCD, namely, the Conference of Heads of State, the Council of Ministers, the Secretariat-General and the Court of Arbitration.

Taken as a whole, the provisions of the Treaty are potentially very far-reaching. Their full implementation would imply a high level of regional economic integration. The combination of fiscal compensation, a system of incentive harmonisation and other envisaged measures such as a regional industrial programme could not only foster a rational pattern of economic specialisation, but also go far to ensure that the economic interests of all member states would be broadly served by integration – which UDAO and UDEAO were unable to do. Even so, it is doubtful whether the Community can be expected to make a significant contribution to promoting the balanced economic development of the member states, in the sense of reducing the existing wide disparities of income and growth. The circumstances of the least developed members suggest that, for them, any prospect of a substantial reduction in income disparities is more likely to be dependent on mineral discovery and exploitation or on substantial inflows of foreign aid aimed at their agricultural improvement, than on the contribution of Community measures themselves, useful as these could be in promoting their industrialisation and more balanced economic structures.

TRADE LIBERALISATION AND THE TCR

It is evident that the Community sets out to be much more than a simple trade bloc. One of its priority objectives is nevertheless to promote intra-group trade. From this point of view, the TCR is clearly a pivotal feature. The TCR is not an entirely novel kind of integration preference. Indeed, it is remarkably similar to the *taxe unique* of the UDEAC (Robson, 1968). The precise form it has taken in the Community, however, and in particular its automatic link with fiscal compensation for concomitant revenue losses, makes it unique. Eligibility for the benefits of the regime is not automatic. The level of the TCR is separately determined for each enterprise, product and country by the Council of Ministers, and that body only considers applications that are put forward by the government of the country in which the enterprise seeking TCR status is domiciled.

The adoption of the TCR was initially slow, but by 1977 the process was well advanced and, by June 1979, a total of 361 approvals had been granted to 188 enterprises for 472 products or groups of products. Of these enterprises, 101 were located in Ivory Coast, 11 in Upper Volta, 12 in Mali, 1 in Mauretania, 5 in Niger and 58 in Senegal (CEAO, 1980). The approvals granted up to 1979 covered most of the Community's industrial products satisfying the rules of origin, and thus eligible to be considered for TCR treatment. The principal exception – and it is a large one – affected trade between Ivory Coast and Senegal. Much of this trade until 1979 remained outside the TCR regime as a result of a bilateral trade agreement inherited from UDEAO, which was allowed to continue for the initial five years of CEAO's operation.

Although the Treaty lays down no principles for determining the levels of the TCR, certain guidelines have been adopted by the Secretariat in formulating its own recommendations to the Council and these are often reflected in the rates established. First, in order to reduce the competitive disadvantages of the least developed member states, TCR rates on their products are often fixed at lower levels than those imposed on the similar products of Ivory Coast and Senegal. Likewise, the land-locked countries and Mauretania often accord lower rates for products traded amongst themselves as compared with rates charged on similar products coming from Ivory Coast and Senegal. Secondly, in order to promote the use of local raw materials and to develop inter-industry linkages, products using local raw materials or locally manufactured intermediate inputs are treated more favourably than products utilising foreign-produced inputs. A third relevant consideration is the presence or absence of a domestic

Table 4.3 CEAO: Absolute Margins of TCR Preference for Selected Products Including those of Major Importance in Intra-State Trade. Tax Rates as at July 1978 (%)

CEAO nomenclature no.	Products	Ivory Coast 1	2	3	Upper Volta 1	2	3	Mali 1	2	3	Mauretania 1	2	3	Niger 1	2	3	Senegal 1	2	3
	I. Food, drink & tobacco																		
19.08.40	Dry biscuits	48	M23 S40	25 8	86	M23 37	63 49	80	55	25	78	12	66	30	27	3	72	36	36
20.02.11	Coffee extract	—	—	—	51	18	33	96	42	38	96	28	68	54	26	28	72	19	53
20.03.02	Beer	54	24	30	109	67	42	103	UV68 76	31 23	103	47	56	51	48	3	72	29	43
24.02.31	Cigarettes	2,425 fr/kg	1,250 fr/kg	1,175 fr/kg	90 +1,500 fr/kg	45	45 .283	105	178	105	105	26 +98 ou/kg		156	28 +1,284 fr/kg		101	38	63
	II. Chemical products																		
34.01.02	Soap	—	—	—	113	79 N34	34 79	99	N50 IC64	30 16	99	12	87	73	41	32	72	32	40
27.10	Lubricating oil	46	40	6	57	35	22	58	3 +14,850 fr/tn	16	58	32	26	32	34	(*)	60	41	19
	III. Plastic products																		
39.02.25	Plastic tubes	48	23	25	38	15	23	25	S18 16	(*) 0	25	UV12 16	13 9	14	15	(*)	60	UV24 IC29	36 31
39.07	Bags	—	—	—	80	50	30	19	UV16	8 11	78	32	46	51	42	9	72	37	35
39.07.60	Household utensils	—	—	—	80	50	30	78	38 IC,S65	30 3	78	29 UV37	49 41	51	38 IC,S42	13 9	72	37	35
39.01.39	Polyurethene foam	48	23	25	—	—	—	35	16	6	35	12	23	19	13	6	60	18	42
	IV. Rubber products																		
40.11.31	Cycle inner tubes	61	UV24 M27	37 34	44	IC18 M16	26 28	105	IC34 UV30	21 25	105	IC32 UV12 M22	73 93 83	76	IC39 26	37 50	72	IC37 19	35 53
40.11.51	Cycle tyres (new)	61	24	37	—	—	—	105	30	25	105	12	93	76	26	50	72	19	53

Product	1	2	3	1	2	3	1	2	3	1	2	3	1	2	3	1	2	3
V Leather & travel goods																		
41.02	36	24	12	77	27	50	68	34	34	65	30	35	38	33	5	—	—	—
VI. Wood products																		
44.15.20 Plywood	—	—	—	56	23	33	49	25	24	65	27	38	39	34	5	60	18	42
94.03.50 Wooden furniture	61	32	29	86	38	48	74	44	30	96	34	62	45	32	13	102	IC32 / UV19	70 / 83
VII. Paper																		
48.16 Cardboard boxes	54	37	17	86	37	49	61	16	45	72	32	40	45	41	4	60	30	30
VIII. Textile products																		
55.05.90 Cotton thread	48	23	25	92	40	52	61	42	19	81	M26	55	54	M37	17	60	N25	35
(other)											N38	43		39	15		18	42
55.09.02 Unbleached cotton cloth	54	24	30	56	0	56	68	30	38	49	M12	37	30	20	10	72	IC26	46
											N27	22					19	19
																		53
61.01.04 Clothing	67	24	43	75	45	30	105	74	31	92	30	62	64	36	28	72	19	53
IX. Footwear																		
64.02 Leather shoes	54	37	17	86	52	34	93	UV43	50	72	UV19	53	45	39	6	72	IC36	36
		UV29	25					65	28		32	40					UV20	52
		47	7					74	19		32	46					36	36
64.01 Plastic shoes	54	47	7	104	64	40	93	74	19	78	32	46	51	45	6	72	36	36
X. Metal products																		
73.38.21 Enamel household goods	54	30	24	58	24	34	74	50	24	78	24	54	25	M14	11	72	32	40
		M24	30		M12	46					M0	78		18	7			
XI. Mechanical industry																		
87.12.10 Vehicle parts, cycles	36	24	12	63	18	45	22	16	6	78	12	66	51	39	12	60	IC22	38
																	N18	42
87.12.60 Vehicle parts, other	61	24	37	63	30	33	43	34	9	78	24	54	51	39	12	60	IC22	38
																	N18	42

Column headings 1, 2 and 3 denote:

1 normal import rates

2 effective rate under TCR. Where TCR rates differ according to origin, this is indicated with initial letters (IC, UV, M, RM (Mauretania), S) against the special rate. The other (normal) rate applies to all others.

3 preference

* anomaly due to valuation methods

— product is not imported under the TCR regime

Source: CEAO (1980).

product in the importing country similar to that for which another country requests a TCR regime.

The rate differentiation produced by the adoption of these guidelines is so far the principal practical manifestation of CEAO's expressed concern with balanced and coordinated industrial development. The absolute levels established for the TCR necessarily also reflect the varying levels of import duty that are imposed in member countries as well as their levels of internal indirect taxation, which, of course, remain applicable to CEAO imports, since these two tax charges jointly determine the effective preference against third countries that any given rate of TCR provides. In this connection it may be noted that, on the whole, Senegal, Upper Volta and Mauretania impose relatively high tariffs, whilst those of Ivory Coast and Mali are more moderate and that of Niger is low.

The preferences *vis-à-vis* third countries that have been established in CEAO under the TCR by the application of these considerations are naturally very disparate but, as shown by Table 4.3, they are commonly substantial, resulting in a TCR rate of some 40–60 per cent of the corresponding effective import duty charge. In a small number of cases, the preferences are much higher, resulting in one or two instances in abatements of the order of 90 per cent. In yet other cases only very modest preferences of the order of 10 per cent have been conceded to Community products, sometimes reflecting the existence of a competing domestic industry in the importing country, which cannot be exposed to the full force of competition in the combined market if it is to survive.

INTRA-CEAO TRADE

The pattern of recorded trade amongst the CEAO countries that accompanies the arrangements just described may next be considered. Aggregate data on recorded trade among CEAO countries are unreliable, in part because of the inconsistent treatment of transit items. Dependable statistics are available only for intra-Community exchanges of manufactured products. Tables 4.4 and 4.5 relate to such exchanges, irrespective of whether the products benefit from the TCR regime. It can be seen that in 1976 total trade in manufactured products amounted to some 20,000 m.fr. CFA. Of this total, Ivory Coast and Senegal jointly accounted for about 98 per cent of total intra-group exports, and trade between those two countries themselves amounted to about a quarter of this component of total intra-Community trade. Both Ivory Coast and Senegal enjoyed substantial favourable trade balances on their intra-Community trade in manu-

Table 4.4 CEAO: Intra-Community Trade in Industrial Products, 1976 (m.fr.CFA)

Imports by / Imports from	Ivory Coast	Upper Volta	Mali	Mauretania	Niger	Senegal	Total
Ivory Coast	–	2,107	4,161	232	1,195	2,621	10,316
Upper Volta	161	–	2	–	30	1	194
Mali	136	27	–	8	–	11	182
Mauretania	1	–	(.)	–	–	2	4
Niger	43	10	5	–	–	–	58
Senegal	2,697	250	2,990	3,913	180	––	10,030
Total	3,038	2,394	7,158	4,153	1,405	2,636	20,784

(.) less than half unit shown.
Source: Adapted from table prepared by Secretariat on the basis of trade statistics of member states.

Table 4.5   *CEAO: Intra-Community Trade Balances in Manufactured Products, 1976 (m.fr.CFA)*

Country	Exports	Imports	Balance
Ivory Coast	10,316	3,038	+7,278
Upper Volta	194	2,394	−2,200
Mali	182	7,158	−6,976
Mauretania	4	4,153	−4,149
Niger	58	1,405	−1,347
Senegal	10,030	2,636	+7,394
Total	20,784	20,784	—

Source: Adapted from CEAO (1978).

factures, whereas the other countries incurred varying but substantial deficits. Between Ivory Coast and Senegal, trade in manufactures was roughly in balance.

Of particular interest is the part of intra-Community trade in manufactures that is subject to TCR. Table 4.6 summarises the value of this trade for the period 1976–8. For 1978 the total value of imports subject to the TCR amounted to 7,886 m. fr. The principal importer was Niger, which accounted for about 31 per cent of the total, followed by Mali, which accounted for 27 per cent, and Upper Volta whose share was about a quarter. The two more advanced members, Ivory Coast and Senegal, accounted for relatively modest shares of these imports, namely, 6.9 and 4.6 per cent respectively – a result attributable to the aforementioned exclusion from the TCR regime until 1 January 1979 of bilateral trade between those two countries under an agreement that antedates the establishment of the CEAO. Excluded trade amounted to a very high proportion of total intra-group trade in manufactures and a still higher proportion of trade potentially eligible for TCR treatment. From 1979 this trade has been formally incorporated into the TCR system.

The commodity composition of intra-Community trade in products subject to the TCR is set out in Table 4.7. It can be seen that, in 1978, cotton thread and cloth accounted for about a quarter of the trade, while coffee extract and lubricating oil, of roughly equal importance, jointly accounted for between a fifth and a quarter of the total. The remaining products traded were quite diverse. The more important categories are plastic products, vehicle parts, household enamel ware, footwear, cigarettes, bicycle tyres and tubes, biscuits, beer and plywood. The enumerated product groups accounted in 1978 for

Table 4.6 *CEAO: Intra-Community Trade in Manufactured Products Subject to the TCR Regime. Value and Revenue Loss (m.fr.CFA)*

Imports by → Exports from	Ivory Coast[a] Value	Ivory Coast[a] Revenue loss	Upper Volta Value	Upper Volta Revenue loss	Mali Value	Mali Revenue loss	Mauretania Value	Mauretania Revenue loss	Niger Value	Niger Revenue loss	Senegal Value	Senegal Revenue loss	Total[a] Value	Total[a] Revenue loss
1976														
Ivory Coast		..	764	265	537	111	12	4	763	117	36	10	(2,112)	
Upper Volta	(57)	32	—	—	—	—	—	—	2	..	—	—	(59)	
Mali	(3)	2	19	13	—	—	—	—	6	1	—	—	(28)	
Mauretania	—	—	—	—	—	—	—	—	—	—	—	—	—	
Niger	—	—	—	—	—	—	—	—	—	—	—	—	—	
Senegal	(100)	4	150	51	276	27	383	141	131	16	—	—	(1,040)	
Total	(160)	38	933	329	814	138	395	144	901	135	36	10	(3,239)	..
1977														
Ivory Coast		..	1,046	389	1,370	262	108	36	1,476	253	346	233	4,346	1,173
Upper Volta	85	31	—	—	—	—	—	—	7	2	—	—	92	33
Mali	4	2	21	14	—	—	—	—	—	—	—	—	25	16
Mauretania	—	—	—	—	—	—	—	—	—	—	—	—	—	—
Niger	—	—	—	—	—	—	—	—	—	—	—	—	—	—
Senegal	47	5	169	57	330	30	465	192	238	28	—	—	1,251	312
Total	137	38	1,236	460	1,700	292	573	229	1,721	283	346	233	5,713	1,534
1978														
Ivory Coast		..	1,736	629	1,703	332	37	14	2,252	332	360	242	6,087	1,549
Upper Volta	210	77	—	—	19	2	—	—	8	—	1	(.)	238	80
Mali	72	20	29	20	—	—	—	—	3	1	4	3	109	44
Mauretania	—	—	—	—	—	—	—	—	—	—	—	—	—	—
Niger	—	—	—	—	—	—	—	—	—	—	—	—	—	—
Senegal	263	67	222	65	409	28	356	160	202	15	—	—	1,452	335
Total	546	165	1,987	715	2,131	363	393	174	2,464	347	364	245	7,886	2,008

[a] For 1976, the Ivory Coast's imports were not included in the source cited. They have been inserted in brackets from estimates separately prepared.

.. not available.

(.) less than half the unit shown.

Source: CEAO (1979c).

Table 4.7 *CEAO: Principal Components of Intra-Community Trade, 1978. Products Subject to the TCR*

Product	Value (m.fr.CFA)	% of total	Principal sources
Cotton cloth	1,573	20.2	Ivory Coast, Senegal, Mali
Coffee extract	872	11.1	Ivory Coast
Lubricating oil	872	11.1	Ivory Coast, Senegal
Cotton thread	431	5.5	Ivory Coast, Senegal
Plastics	347	4.4	Ivory Coast
Vehicle parts	278	3.5	Ivory Coast
Household enamel ware	275	3.5	Senegal, Ivory Coast
Footwear	273	3.4	Senegal, Ivory Coast
Cigarettes	262	3.3	Ivory Coast, Senegal
Bicycle tyres & tubes	231	2.9	Upper Volta
Biscuits	230	2.9	Ivory Coast, Senegal
Beer	192	2.4	Ivory Coast
Plywood	162	2.1	Ivory Coast
Total of categories listed above	5,998	76.2	
Total intra-Community trade subject to the TCR	7,886	100.0	

Source: CEAO (1979c).

three-quarters of intra-group trade in TCR products. In almost every case the principal sources of supply were Ivory Coast and Senegal.

INTER-COUNTRY AND INTRA-INDUSTRIAL PRODUCT SPECIALISATION IN CEAO

The extent to which the emergent pattern of trade and specialisation in CEAO is appropriate to the relative opportunity costs of the different producers and the distributional constraints imposed by the member states is at present impossible to determine. In terms of nominal 'revealed comparative advantage' as indicated by market performance in non-preferential third markets, the Ivory Coast and Senegal both clearly enjoy productive superiority over their neighbours. In part, however, that performance reflects distortions that are produced by their investment incentives – as does the performance of those countries within the Community.

Although systematic evidence on relative real opportunity costs of production for all Community countries is not at present available, for Ivory Coast, Senegal and Mali, in the early 1970s some indications may be extracted from World Bank studies (Balassa, 1978) on incentives and resource costs. These studies suggest that Senegal and Ivory Coast differ in their respective productive efficiencies in different sectors, but that both are superior to Mali, thus broadly confirming both the potential gains to be derived from integration despite important similarities in the resource base of member countries, as well as the natural economic dominance of the two coastal states.

But the pattern of trade and specialisation in CEAO is influenced not only by comparative advantage, the TCR and the impact of national investment incentives, but also to an undetermined but certainly important extent by the policies of transnational enterprises that are dominant in the industrial and manufacturing sectors. A number of these enterprises are involved in several countries of the Community, in part (as in textiles) through interlocking financial participations.

One very notable feature of industrial development in CEAO is the lack of specialisation. There is little inter-country specialisation on particular products, little specialisation on product ranges and little intra-industry trade between countries. In most sectors of industry, plants are replicated and production therefore takes place on a smaller scale and a less specialised basis than the size and structure of the regional market would permit, even allowing for the importance of transport costs in limiting the scope for profitable specialisation in this vast Community. As a result, the advantages of integration that derive from specialisation and the exploitation of scale economies are certainly dissipated. Uneconomic replication has occurred notably in textiles (despite the interlocking links of many of the enterprises involved), and also in batteries, pharmaceuticals and plastics. Only in a few industries does a limited degree of product specialisation occur – as in footwear, where Bata does not produce a complete range at each of its plants.

A strikingly similar lack of industrial specialisation is also found in the Central African grouping of UDEAC, where the *taxe unique* operates in a similar way to the TCR, and where a number of the same transnational corporations (TNCs) also operate – Bata, Riegel, Schaeffer, CFAO, and so on. Despite important differences between the two integration arrangements (Robson, 1968), the outcomes, in terms of limited trade and lack of specialisation, have been remarkably similar. In UDEAC too, market segmentation is widespread, and plants and products are replicated throughout the region.

The segmentation of the UDEAC market has recently been severely criticised in a report presented to the Annual Conference of the UDEAC Council of Heads of State (UN Economic Commission for Africa, 1981), which attributes the lack of specialisation to the operations of transnational corporations. Their activities are condemned as unconstructive and as constituting a disintegrative, rather than an integrative, force in the regional economy. Intra-regional trade flows are claimed to respond not so much to conditions in the UDEAC countries as to the global and regional strategies adopted by these firms which are seen as the beneficiaries of intra-regional trade (p. 80). The single tax system is said to have facilitated the restructuring of UDEAC markets by TNCs in such a way as to limit intra-industrial specialisation and hence the growth of intra-regional trade. This has occurred by the extensive use of variable single tax rates to segment the regional market into separate national markets, within each of which an oligopolistic, or in some instances, a monopolistic market structure is created (p. 89). By segmenting the UDEAC market into separate national markets, by promoting duty-free imports of capital goods, raw materials and intermediate products, by providing tax holidays and other inducements that artificially cheapen the cost of capital, the single tax system and the common investment code have, it is contended, strengthened the market dominance of foreign-owned companies, have guaranteed their profitability, have eliminated incentives to efficient production and have encouraged replication of plants and products throughout the region. In short, TNCs have thwarted efforts at regional industrial planning (p. 97). It is conceded that TNCs might nevertheless provide net benefits to the host countries (p. 80). A convincing evaluation of benefits could, of course, only be undertaken on a firm by firm basis. Nevertheless, despite its failure to provide evidence on the central issue of benefits, the report is condemnatory in tone. Its unqualified conclusion is that the revenue-poor states derive little benefit from the transnational corporations that locate subsidiaries within their borders.

Are such judgements valid, or are the criticisms misplaced? Would they apply also to CEAO? Certainly experience in the two economic groupings in relation to industrial development has been remarkably similar, and industrial development in both groupings has overwhelmingly resulted from the operations of a handful of large multinational corporations, each of which possesses alternative investment options elsewhere and much bargaining power. Nevertheless, to attribute the less than optimal outcome principally to the multinationals seems to be misplaced. The root of the difficulties lies in the failure of the two economic groupings to agree on programmes of planned regional specialisation. The TCR and the *taxe unique* of UDEAC are devices that enable member states – in particular the less developed ones – to protect themselves to some extent from the consequences of this failure. The outcome is unquestionably market fragmentation, but the less than ideal conduct of the multinationals from the standpoint of the Community, and even from the standpoint of the host countries themselves, is essentially their opportunistic response to the lack of a coherent regional industrialisation strategy.

It is also true that distortions induced by the kinds of national investment incentives offered to investors, including duty-free importation of intermediate products, discourage the development of local linkages. This is again a matter that the member countries are competent to remedy if they choose, though for maximum effect their actions must be coordinated at Community level. It does not, of course, follow that the elimination of such distortions will necessarily suffice to deal fully with this and related problems resulting from the operations of transnationals, as the literature summarised by Kirkpatrick and Nixson (1981, p. 391 et seq.) reminds us, but their impact should be much reduced.

In any case, what is the alternative? It is not, surely, the ideal situation, in which restrictions are totally absent, but more probably a total fragmentation of the market in which even present gains, modest as they doubtless are, would be wholly forgone. Some of the valid criticisms levelled in the ECA report against the policy-makers in UDEAC are demonstrably less applicable to CEAO. For instance, in the latter, TCR rates can be and have been adjusted to encourage the utilisation of local inputs – although the differences are often relatively small by comparison with the large benefits that may be derived from the duty-free importation of intermediates and capital goods.

It is of the utmost importance, in any event, that each country should properly evaluate its interests in relation to initiatives from foreign investors, and should not concede levels of fiscal and other concessions that cannot be justified by reference to social cost–benefit evaluations and other broader, relevant considerations. In this connection, however, it would be inappropriate to look solely at the revenues forgone through tax holidays. The evaluation of UDEAC by the UN Economic Commission for Africa comes near to doing so in its assertion that 'The real fiscal loss from the single tax system is . . . the . . . revenues forgone through tax holidays' (1981, p. 81). This may be so if a naive view of the net welfare gain associated with direct foreign investment is taken, namely, that it will be determined principally by the authorities' additional revenues from profits taxation, as in one version of the model formulated by MacDougall (1960). In the context of UDEAC and CEAO, such a view would be of little or no policy significance.

In the end, the uneconomic replication of industries in CEAO is principally the result of constraints imposed by government policies in the individual member countries. The only issue is the framework within which those constraints and their formation are to be explained. But whatever conclusion is reached in this respect, the importance of the risk factor as perceived by entrepreneurs should not be underrated. Even within the constraints of the present limited framework of regional economic cooperation, a greater degree of specialisation would often be privately profitable if the stability of the Community market could be relied on. The longer it survives, the greater may be the disposition to assume that it will continue. But the fact is that, in the event of disruption of the regional market, the purely domestic markets of the smaller, least developed members of the Community would be far too small to absorb the output of a large plant limited to a narrow range of intermediate or final products. The risk of disruption is a factor that will inevitably continue to affect the operation of CEAO for some time to come. In the absence of a convincing industrialisation policy, its impact can be overcome only by potentially expensive investment incentives.

FISCAL COMPENSATION AND THE DISTRIBUTION OF COSTS AND BENEFITS

One significant feature that differentiates the CEAO from its two predecessors – UDAO and UDEAO – is the provision made in the former for the payment of fiscal compensation for revenue losses. These provisions represent an attempt to alleviate important problems that typically arise in customs unions and economic groupings. At a general level these were discussed in Chapter 3.

The need for some such measures – though not necessarily of the specific form found in CEAO – arises because economic integration among developing countries usually generates distributional problems, which, if not remedied, may ultimately disrupt the bloc (as happened with the predecessors of CEAO). The problems have three sources. First, the static costs of trade diversion often fall disproportionately on the least developed members. Secondly, the least developed members may also be exposed to net adjustment costs and, indeed, to enduring costs from trade creation if, unlike the case assumed in the neoclassical theory of integration, resources are immobile and unemployment exists. Thirdly, disproportionate costs may arise – for the least developed members in particular – from the reduction in their freedom to protect new industries because of the constraints imposed by tariff and other policy harmonisation measures. These problems are all present in CEAO.

These problems of balance and equity will not be entirely resolved without an effective regional policy, perhaps embodying administrative control over industrial development and its location, or at any rate without the adoption of market instruments of similar effect. CEAO has, however, tried to alleviate the specific problem of imbalance in the costs of trade liberalisation by resort to fiscal compensation.

The approach in CEAO is to pay fiscal compensation by reference to revenue losses arising in the process of trade liberalisation. The rationale of compensation is nevertheless not to offset revenue losses *per se*, since these could in principle be overcome by the imposition of alternative non-discriminatory internal indirect taxes, but to offset the impact or static costs of trade diversion, which themselves represent losses of national income. These costs arise when, as a result of trade preferences, imports from a member country replace imports from a lower-cost source outside the group. If then, because of polarised economic development and wide disparities in the levels of industrial development of the participants, intra-group trade is markedly unbalanced, as it is in CEAO, a convincing case for compensation can be made out and there is justification for basing it on revenue losses (Robson, 1980, pp. 179–80).

Fiscal compensation in CEAO is payable to member states in respect of the revenue losses deemed to be incurred as a result of the provision of intra-Community preferences under the TCR. These losses are defined as the difference between the duties that would be imposed on a product imported from a third country not subject to the *droit de douane* and the duties imposed under the TCR regime. The *droit de douane* is a relatively small component – now 5 per cent – of the aggregate fiscal import duties charged by the members of CEAO and was in effect the means by which a two-column tariff was operated.

The required interbudgetary transfers are effected through the Community Development Fund (FCD). The Treaty provides for compensation as of right to be paid to each member state to the extent of two-thirds of its assessed losses. A further amount equal to one-third of the aggregate assessed losses is distributed on a discretionary basis among member states to support national development projects of Community interest. The distribution of this discretionary part of FCD is determined by the Conference of Heads of State. For the initial five-year period, it was decided to distribute it

Table 4.8 CEAO: Community Development Fund, 1976 (m.fr.CFA)

Country	Estimated intra-CEAO industrial exports		Contribution to moins-value	Estimated receipts						Estimated net contribution (+) or receipts (−)	
				Fiscal compensation		Support for development projects		Total amount receivable			As % of budget revenue
	Value	% of total		Amount	% of total	Amount	% of total	Amount	% of total	Amount	
Ivory Coast	15,700.1	60.8	1,385.7	403.8	26.6	—	—	403.8	18.6	+981.9	0.7
Upper Volta	341.5	1.3	30.1	421.2	27.7	206.6	31.8	627.8	28.9	−597.7	3.3
Mali	403.0	1.6	35.6	122.4	8.1	206.6	31.8	329.0	15.2	−293.4	1.3
Mauretania	1.6	(0.008)	0.2	229.2	19.7	76.1	11.7	375.3	17.3	−375.1	(1.6)
Niger	110.3	(0.4)	9.7	146.7	9.6	160.7	24.7	307.4	14.2	−297.7	1.4
Senegal	9,282.9	35.9	819.3	126.9	8.3	—	—	126.9	5.8	+692.4	0.9
	25,839.4	100.0	2,280.6	1,520.2	100.0	650.0	100.0	2,170.2	100.0	+110.4	

Note: 15% of the one-third of *moins-value* allocated to national development projects (= 110.4m.fr.) is retained for reserve or other purposes.

Source: Derived from initial Secretariat forecasts of industrial exports, and of trade in manufactures subject to the TCR.

solely amongst the least industrialised members, that is, Niger, Upper Volta, Mauretania and Mali, according to a coefficient that reflected their relative GNP *per capita* (1976 Acte No. 12/76; CEAO, *Journal Officiel*, No. 3, 1976).

Table 4.8 illustrates the forecasted operation of FCD for 1976, based on the Secretariat's initial estimates of trade and of revenue losses. On this basis it can be seen that the operations of FCD in 1976 would have resulted in a net redistribution of fiscal resources towards the least developed member states of some 1.5 b. fr.CFA. Two-thirds of the transfer would have been in the form of an untied budgetary transfer, whilst the remaining one-third would have taken the form of earmarked payments to support specified national development projects. For 1976, national development projects so supported included equipment for customs services, urban water supply, animal health projects and industrial promotion centres.

Redistributional operations on this scale are not of major budgetary significance for the member states. For the two net contributory countries, namely, Ivory Coast and Senegal, the calculated contributions are equivalent to some 0.7 per cent and 0.9 per cent of their respective ordinary budgets in the year in question. For the recipients, the calculated amounts receivable are more significant, being equivalent in total to 3.3 per cent of budgetary revenue in the case of Upper Volta, 1.3 per cent for Mali and 1.4 per cent for Niger. Ivory Coast's net contribution was equivalent to about 6.3 per cent of the value of its total industrial exports to the Community and for Senegal the corresponding figure was 7.5 per cent. The contribution to balance and integration that could have been made by the FCD would be modest.

The initial estimates proved to be overoptimistic and the sums initially available for discretionary compensation turned out to be much smaller than anticipated. Recognition of the limited contribution that could be made to the promotion of balance by the operation of FCD on its own thus led the heads of state at their meeting at Bamako in October 1978 to agree to establish an additional instrument of economic cooperation in the shape of a Solidarity Fund (le Fonds de Solidarité et d'Intervention pour le Développement de la Communauté Economique de l'Afrique de l'Ouest – FOSIDEC) (Protocol 'M'). The object of FOSIDEC is to promote the economic development of member states and to contribute to the regional balance of the Community by means of loans, guarantees, subsidies, participations and feasibility studies. In its activities, FOSIDEC is required to give priority to the least developed member states. For the initial two-year period 1977–8, FOSIDEC was financed by capital contributions from member states amounting to 5,000 m. fr.CFA.

Subsequently FOSIDEC was to receive aggregate annual contributions of 1500 m. fr.CFA.

For the initial period of its operations, until 1983, the Fund will not undertake lending activities but will be used to provide guarantees (up to ten times the contribution of members). Contributions are placed on deposit and the interest is used, after covering the costs of administration, to finance feasibility studies and to subsidise the interest costs of borrowers from other sources by up to one-third of the rate charged. Since the effective commencement of operations in 1979, a number of guarantees have been provided for projects in Mauretania, Niger and Senegal. Interest rate subsidies have also commenced. Several feasibility studies have been financed. By December 1979, member states had contributed 5,700m. fr., and 800m. fr. was outstanding. The intervention fund available to finance studies and subsidies then stood at 600m. fr. (FOSIDEC, 1980). In conjunction with the FCD, the establishment of FOSIDEC equips CEAO with an institutional basis for compensation and development that is comparable in scope with the ECOWAS Fund for Cooperation, Compensation and Development. It could usefully supplement the otherwise modest resources for promoting the development of the least developed members of the group, although the extent of their priority in FOSIDEC's operations remains to be seen.

The operations of FCD itself would have been much larger during the initial quinquennium than they were but for the treatment accorded to trade between Senegal and Ivory Coast, much of which took place free of duties under a bilateral agreement dating from 1971. A decision of the heads of state in 1973 effectively excluded this bilaterial trade from the creation of *moins-value* or compensation payments during the period in question, although it was included in the base used for determining relative contributions to FCD. This arrangement was not extended on its expiry on 1 January 1979. From that date onwards, trade between Senegal and Ivory Coast will result in *moins-value* and compensation payments to the extent that preferences are granted under the TCR. If, as this trade became incorporated in the TCR, the previous arrangements had otherwise continued, the amounts available for discretionary redistribution through FCD to the least developed members would have been substantially enlarged. However, with the integration of this previously excluded trade into the Community's regular compensatory operations (at the insistence of the partners of Ivory Coast and Senegal), a revised basis was simultaneously introduced for dealing with that part of FCD's receipts (one-third in all) that is not automatically applied to compensation for revenue losses and that, in principle, is available for discretionary redistributive payments via support for approved projects. The distributive effects of these changes are not yet clear, but since Ivory Coast and Senegal have become eligible for payments from this source, the benefits that the least developed countries might otherwise have received from additional earmarked payments are likely to be reduced, although they could still be substantial. It appears even so that, if fully implemented, CEAO's fiscal arrangements during the first five years should have compensated Niger, Upper Volta, Mali and Mauretania directly or indirectly to the extent of more than 100 per cent of their calculated revenue losses.

An assessment of whether these or any other similar arrangements could be viewed as equitable must obviously depend not merely on their purely *fiscal* or financial effects, but also on their *economic* implications, for it is these that determine the resulting distribution of the burdens and benefits of the operation.

If such a compensation arrangement is judged purely in terms of the extent to which it resolves the problem of the static costs of trade diversion, a major consideration must evidently be how the prices of the products enjoying preferential treatment are affected as a result of the preferences. If export prices should rise fully to reflect the tariff preferences, exporting countries would not lose real income but might lose disposable public revenue through their need to make provision for the fiscal transfers. The rise in the taxable incomes of exporters, if it could be taxed, would to some degree offset this. Those countries that are net importers would for their part require substantially full compensation for revenue losses if their public revenues (and real national incomes) were not to be reduced by preferential trade, as compared with their positions under a non-discriminatory tariff (whether this is the appropriate *anti-monde* for evaluating the costs and benefits of an integration arrangement is, perhaps, debatable). If, perhaps more realistically, it is assumed that the prices of exports do not rise by the full amount of the preference, in either the short or long run, then exporting countries would bear some of the real, as well as the fiscal, burden of compensation and, at the same time, the 'static' argument for providing importing countries with full compensation in respect of preferential imports would fall away.

In the case of CEAO, such comparisons require further qualification since compensation payments and receipts are related to a purely theoretical and lower measure of preference that is calculated by reference to import duties after excluding the *droit de douane*. Yet the bulk of the Community's imports come from the European Economic Community (EEC), whose products are now subject to that levy to varying extents. The specified basis of calculation will thus tend to benefit net exporting countries at the expense of net importing countries. Upper Volta was a special case because, until the implementation of the fiscal reforms to be discussed in the concluding section, its revenue losses have been calculated by reference to an import duty tariff that implicitly included internal indirect taxes.

In a broader perspective, other considerations may be important, if not decisive. Preferential trade arrangements do not merely result in the reallocation of a given volume of trade, but should also generate trade expansion. If an exporting country does not merely sell existing production at a higher price, but also expands its output, that country's gains may exceed the value of the preferential margin, because of the resulting benefits from an increase of output and employment. Likewise if, for an importing country, the relevant alternative to importing from a partner is not to import the good from the rest of the world but to produce it domestically, the opportunity costs of imports in real income terms and in terms of broader public objectives forgone may similarly exceed the nominal aggregate value of the preferential margin. To take these factors into account would require an attempt to evaluate the overall costs and benefits of integration. That clearly cannot be undertaken by assessing its impact effects on national income, but would also have to take into account a multiplicity of goals of public policy, including the creation of a more balanced economic structure, modernisation and economic stability.

At the stage presently reached by CEAO, many of these broader considerations do not come into play. This is not, of course, to say that they are not important policy objectives, but merely that the Community's trade and customs arrangements have not yet seriously impaired the policy autonomy of any of its least developed members with respect to the attainment of these objectives. This is principally because levels of tariff protection are not yet uniform and also because the degree of intra-Community preference accorded to partners through the TCR is, in any case, a matter for negotiation. From this perspective, at least for the period to 1979, CEAO's formal fiscal arrangements might be said to represent a not unsatisfactory arrangement for its least developed members, but it must be emphasised that this is a very limited standpoint. Moreover, if tariffs and other policy instruments become harmonised, an entirely different situation would be created. But in any case, the compensation arrangements outlined have not operated entirely as planned. They are under strain and increasing difficulties are being experienced as the budgetary problems of the members become more acute. Administrative difficulties arose in the first place over obtaining the trade data for determining claims. Furthermore, member states have been tardy in paying their contributions and, in some cases even, in claiming benefits. These difficulties account for the failure to close the FCD account for 1976 until 1981, while the FCD for 1980 will not be closed until 1985. As a result, the actual payments made during the initial quinquennium may, in the end, turn out not to be sufficient fully to compensate the poorer importing members of the Community for their 'revenue' losses.

There is little prospect at present that the constraints affecting the Fund will soon be overcome. For 1981 the FCD was fixed at 6,760.2m. fr. of which 4,506.8m. represented the two-thirds amount for automatic compensation and the balance of 2,253.4m. fr. represented the one-third balance available to finance activities of Community interest. Of this sum, the Ivory Coast was to contribute 57.4 per cent, calculated on the basis of its industrial exports, and the corresponding share of Senegal was fixed at 38.9 per cent. However, the contribution of the one-third element was simultaneously deferred until 1982 (Acte No. 40/80/CE; CEAO, *Journal Officiel*, Nos 3 and 4, 1980).

For 1982 the FCD was fixed at 7,008m. fr., of which 4,672m. related to automatic compensation and the one-third balance of 2,336m. fr. related to the financing of community projects. Of this total, the share of Ivory Coast had risen to 73.9 per cent while that of Senegal had fallen to 19.9 per cent. Once again, however, the contributions of the one-third element were postponed until 1983 (CEAO, *Journal Officiel*, Nos 3 and 4, 1981).

Against a background of budgetary difficulties in the contributory states and the problem of collecting contributions, CEAO is giving consideration to alternative methods of financing both the FCD and also FOSIDEC. Echoing the EEC itself, the Community now appears to be thinking in terms of providing itself with its 'own' resources, and it has drawn up the terms of reference for a broad study of alternative methods of financing the Community through the institution of a community solidarity tax (Taxe Communautaire de Solidarité – TCS) to replace wholly or partly the annual contributions now made by member states to finance CEAO and FOSIDEC.

PROGRESS AND PROBLEMS

The decade that has elapsed since the Treaty of Abidjan came into force provides a convenient timespan to assess the progress that has been made towards the implementation of the provisions of the Treaty and the attainment of general Community goals, and to review the principal problems now confronting the Community.

Substantial progress has clearly been made towards implementing the Treaty's provisions in the field of customs affairs. A common customs and statistical nomenclature has been adopted and those provisions of the Treaty relating to the allocation of revenues of a conventional customs union type appear to be operating satisfactorily. Although a common external tariff (CET) is not yet in sight, agreement has been reached on the introduction of a simplified and harmonised structure for customs duties and other indirect taxes. Each member state has agreed to adopt a uniform *droit de douane* of 5 per cent and a single supplementary fiscal import duty, so bringing the total effective import duty up to the level of the charges previously imposed in diverse form. This measure of simplification clears the way for the ultimate unification of the supplementary fiscal duty to arrive at a CET.

The specified measures for trade liberalisation and trade expansion, involving the duty-free circulation of most *produits du cru* and preferential treatment for industrial products originating in the area, have also been largely implemented and have facilitated a substantial amount of intra-group trade. Although it is impossible to estimate how much is due to Treaty provisions, it is certain that intra-Community trade in manufactures between Ivory Coast and Senegal on the one hand and the less developed members of the Community on the other would not have been as great without the trade preferences.

The related objective of eliminating non-tariff barriers and specifically quantitative restrictions upon intra-group trade has yet to be fully attained. With the possible exception of Upper Volta, which appears to have implemented the relevant provisions of the Treaty in letter and spirit, each member state operates certain trade restrictions in defiance of the provisions of the Treaty and subsequent Council decisions. The restrictions usually take the form of import certificates, which the injured parties claim are not always freely issued. Restrictions of this kind have been particularly prevalent in the textile industry where excess capacity widely exists. Ivory Coast, Senegal, Mali and Niger have all imposed restrictions on textile products. Restrictions have also been imposed on other manufactures including confectionary and pneumatic tyres. Even in the field of *produits du cru*, certain restrictions have been operated. A contentious instance has been Ivory Coast's practice of limiting green coffee exports and of charging higher prices for the exported product than are charged to domestic processors.

The recorded expansion of intra-Community trade in manufactures has undoubtedly been facilitated by fiscal compensation arrangements, which, if fully implemented, would effectively relieve the less developed member states of the real costs of trade diversion. One of the supposed merits of the particular approach adopted is that it avoids any direct link between compensation payments and preference margins received by any state, thus overcoming an obvious constraint to trade liberalisation negotiations. However, since Ivory Coast and Senegal finance the bulk of the required contributions (for 1982, in gross terms, 74 per cent and 20 per cent respectively) and are aware of this, in considering whether to seek the accession of additional products to the TCR regime the implicit additional fiscal costs of doing so can hardly fail to be allowed for. This does appear, at times, to have led to a reluctance on the part of Ivory Coast and Senegal to seek the extension of the system.

The interests of the less developed members with respect to those products that do receive TCR preference should not have suffered from the trade liberalisation provisions of the Treaty, to the extent that they have been compensated for the full cost of trade diversion in the initial five years since the obligations and constraints imposed upon their development policies are so far minimal. At the same time, the two major exporters derive net benefits in terms of an expansion of real domestic income, although probably at some budgetary cost, which they are increasingly reluctant to disregard.

Whether the pattern of intra-group trade that has arisen in CEAO suitably reflects the competitive advantages of the respective producers is, as noted elsewhere (pp 52–3) not easy to determine. In any case, the emergent pattern of specialisation in CEAO is influenced not only by private costs as modified by national investment incentives, but also by the policies of transnational corporations that operate in several countries of the Community. It does not appear that the operations of the transnationals have stimulated intra-industry specialisation within CEAO (p. 53). On the contrary there is a noticeable replication of similar plants, which in some instances results in a dissipation of the economies of regional integration – an outcome for which the risk factor may largely account (p. 56).

If the achievements of CEAO in several policy areas are apparent, its limitations are equally obvious. The Community has grown out of an orthodox trade liberalisation bloc, and its main achievements so far are largely confined to this sphere. Despite the declared intention of its members to broaden the scope of their cooperation and to establish an economic community, there has been little or no progress towards implementing the required measures of positive integration that were outlined in the Treaty. Even with respect to the minimum objective of establishing a uniform degree of external tariff protection, little progress has been made.

A CET was to have been established within twelve years of the coming into force of the Treaty, that is, by January 1985, and this target date has been reaffirmed. It is true that certain preparatory measures have already been adopted, including: the introduction of a common tariff and statistical nomenclature; the simplification of the indirect tax systems and the adoption of a uniform *droit de douane* of 5 per cent. The amount of time that has been necessary to complete these relatively uncontroversial and largely technical changes does not inspire optimism about the larger task of attaining a CET by 1985.

The likely difficulties confronting the elaboration of a comprehensive CET invite consideration of a more limited alternative approach to tariff harmonisation, namely to aim at a CET initially only for those products in which trade is currently significant or is likely to become so shortly. If this approach were followed, the range of required negotiations could be substantially limited and at the same time many of the benefits of integration could just as efficaciously be secured. The Community would retain its present appearance of a (qualified) free trade area to the extent that many tariff positions would continue to differ, but uniformity would be attained for items of Community origin that are significantly traded in the region, which is what is important. Such an approach should be coupled with an agreement requiring tariffs to be harmonised on the products of any new industries as a precondition of their becoming eligible for the TCR regime, and also on crucial imported intermediate inputs.

A sectoral or designated product approach to trade liberalisation of this kind would normally be open to the objection that it might entail allocative distortions in the regional economy. In CEAO, the limited extent of inter-industry linkages suggests that little weight would attach to this point until industrial development and internal integration have been carried a good deal further.

The fundamental purpose of adopting a CET – even if limited to certain designated products – is, of course, to provide a uniform measure of protection to Community industries, so promoting an optimal allocation of resources in the region. But that objective cannot be secured unless domestic fiscal incentives are also harmonised. If this is not done it would be possible for any member state to alter unilaterally the measure of protection effectively afforded by a given tariff. The Treaty of Abidjan provides that its members will seek to harmonise fiscal incentives, and proposals were to have been submitted to the Conference of Heads of State by 1975, but by 1982 this had still not been attempted. Incentive harmonisation is inevitably a sensitive policy area in economic groupings. It is made still more so in CEAO by the constraints on the use of monetary and exchange rate policy that are involved for four of its member states by their membership of the West African Monetary Union. So long as the Community's positive economic activities remain so restricted, there is little likelihood that a comprehensive CET would be welcomed by most members, unless a substantial degree of national autonomy with respect to fiscal incentives is simultaneously retained, at least for sensitive categories of economic activity.

An increasingly apparent weakness of the Community lies in the absence of a regional industrial policy, on which action was supposed to have been taken within three years of the Community's establishment. This is really the crucial issue, for until some agreement in principle is reached on basic issues of industrial policy it is hard to see how constructive advances can be made on either the common external tariff or domestic fiscal incentives, since at Community level incentive policy must reflect industrial policy and give effect to it. In the absence of a regional industrial policy, industrial developments continue to be initiated in member states that largely replicate existing developments in other member states, often in activities such as textiles, to which Mauretania is the most recent entrant, where substantial surplus capacity already exists. Developments of this kind underline the need to give urgent attention to industrial coordination if the basic production and cost gains of combining markets are not to be dissipated.

In other fields of economic cooperation such as agriculture and transport – the latter, incidentally, still notably ill adapted to serve intra-Community trade – progress has been negligible. It is indeed difficult to discern any significant initiatives here of a specific Community, as distinct from a purely national, character. One promising development in the field of higher education and research, however, is that a number of regional institutions have reached the stage of detailed feasibility studies, and external financing for them has been negotiated on a Community basis.

The issues discussed up to this point are specific to CEAO. There are evidently other issues arising from the broader context of CEAO's operations and the policies of certain of its members that demand attention in any appraisal of the prospects of the bloc.

Regional economic integration as expressed by CEAO is necessarily to some extent an inward-looking policy. For the least developed members of the CEAO, there is probably no feasible alternative for some time to come if they wish to accelerate industrialisation and to promote a more balanced economic structure without, at the same time, incurring excessive costs. The prospects may be different for the Ivory Coast, which has a strong record of industrialisation behind it in the past twenty years, and which has already developed a diversified export trade in West Africa outside CEAO. Prospects may conceivably be different also for Senegal. If policy reappraisals were to induce Ivory Coast to adopt a more outward-looking policy – perhaps directed towards the EEC – in the interests of maintaining and accelerating its industrial growth, the changes required in its tariff and incentive system might not be easily compatible with the needs of CEAO. At the very least, the adoption of such a policy might induce Ivory Coast to give less weight in future to the maintenance of its Community links. If CEAO's principal nominal paymaster were to assume such a stance, the cohesion of CEAO could be in jeopardy.

At a wider level, the principal question mark overhanging CEAO concerns its relations with ECOWAS, to which all of its members also belong. Membership of both is acceptable so long as their respective obligations do not conflict. The broad objectives of the two groups are similar, although their specific approaches to particular issues do differ in certain respects. Until recently, there appears to have been little coordination between the two institutions and, despite the overlapping national membership of comparable bodies at official and political levels, policies have at times been shaped by one organisation without taking adequate account of existing or projected measures in the other. For instance, the tariff nomenclatures adopted by each group are similar but not identical; fiscal compensation provisions are similar in objectives and administrative procedures, but are not identical in content, and are not immediately compatible; changes under discussion could only exacerbate the problems; rules of origin are not identical. Some, at least, of these differences constitute important obstacles to the assimilation of the operations of the two groups.

A final question that cannot be avoided is whether there can be a continuing role for CEAO if ECOWAS is successful. In this event, CEAO might find a continued justification in fostering a more intimate form of cooperation amongst its members than could be attained in ECOWAS for many years to come, if ever. But, to make this possible, certain changes would be required of CEAO itself in several fields, including compensation and trade liberalisation. In addition, or alternatively, derogations or waivers from compliance with the Lagos Treaty would have to be sought.

These are questions for the future. For the time being, the economic interests of the member states of CEAO are unlikely to be served by postponing attempts to advance towards more effective and positive regional economic integration amongst themselves. The group's principal members are, however, increasingly beset by pressing domestic economic problems. It remains to be seen whether they will be inclined to try to impart a further impetus to the economic integration of the group – unless perhaps they should be moved by a desire to promote zonal political stability. With memories still fresh of the external intervention experienced by certain West African states in the concluding stages of 1980, it would not be surprising if the political factor were, in future, to play a more supportive role in underpinning the evolution of the group than has so far been the case.

Even in the absence of new initiatives, however motivated, CEAO could survive, for its techniques of cooperation – unlike those adopted in some other blocs, including ECOWAS – are very flexible. Moreoever, they do not essentially depend for their stability on the adoption of further measures of policy harmonisation – unlike the situation in ECOWAS. But it can hardly be disputed that the price of failure to implement the originally envisaged measures of positive economic integration would be a correspondingly limited scope for exploiting its potential gains.

5 The Mano River Union

INTRODUCTION

The Mano River Union was inaugurated in October 1973 between
Liberia and Sierra Leone. The founding members have a common
border and share important ethnic, political and cultural similarities,
which are illuminatingly analysed by Christopher Clapham (1976).
The fluctuating history during the past two decades of their initiatives
for political and economic regional cooperation has been dominated
by the personalities and ideological convictions of their respective
leaders, and by their preoccupation with relationships with their
more immediate African neighbours as distinct from broader African
links, though these have not been disregarded. Liberia and Sierra
Leone had indeed previously been involved in 1964, together with
Ivory Coast and Guinea, in a proposal for a West African free trade
area, but this initiative became a victim of political conflict between
Ivory Coast and Guinea (Sesay, 1980).

At an economic level, current cooperation between the two founding members of the MRU has its roots in initiatives going back to
1967 that had envisaged the introduction of limited trade preferences
for the products of a number of existing industries and cooperation to
promote the establishment of new industries to serve their combined
markets. Negotiations were intensified in 1971, when a joint ministerial committee on economic cooperation was established. In 1972
the two governments invited the United Nations Development Programme to set up a joint mission to study more closely the scope for
cooperation in trade and in agricultural and industrial development
and to advise on an appropriate institutional framework. In its report
(UN Conference on Trade and Development, 1973), the mission
endorsed the benefits to be anticipated from economic cooperation in
trade and development but for this purpose chose to recommend the
institution of a full customs union, with a common external tariff and
complete trade liberalisation for goods of local origin, rather than the
looser arrangements that had been under discussion earlier. The mission's recommendations were endorsed by the joint ministerial committee and on 3 October 1973, on the basis of its proposals, the two
heads of state signed an international convention termed the Mano

River Declaration (MRU, 1976b), in which it was agreed to establish a customs union. Specific arrangements for the MRU were left to be laid down in subsequent protocols, of which, by January 1979, eighteen had been adopted (MRU, 1979). The Mano River bridge, the first tangible symbol of the Union, was completed in 1976. It reduces the distance between the two capitals from over 1,000km to 550km, and so constitutes an important element of infrastructure for promoting trade and relations between the two founding members. The original declaration made provision for the later adherence of other West African states and in October 1980, under the Nineteenth Protocol, Guinea acceded to the Union.

THE ECONOMIES OF THE MEMBER STATES

In 1980, Liberia had a population of 1.9 million and Sierra Leone 3.5 million. Both countries are relatively well endowed with natural resources; iron ore, diamonds and bauxite are already being exported, and rutile mining is under way. Land with agricultural potential is relatively abundant: of Liberia's 24 million acres, only 1.3 million are in use, while of Sierra Leone's available 14.5 million acres, only 1 million are under cultivation. Sierra Leone has good fishing resources and both countries possess extensive forests. Considerable potential exists for hydroelectric power from the Mano River.

Almost uniform ecological conditions in the two countries have produced very similar patterns of agricultural production. Physical and climatic conditions are particularly suitable for tree crops such as cocoa, coffee, rubber and oil palm, which are the principal cash crops. Some plantations exist, notably in Liberia. Agriculture rests on small-scale peasant producers using hand tools and is characterised by low productivity. Rice forms the staple diet, but many other food crops and some vegetables are grown. Only a small part of food crop production is commercialised, the bulk being grown for consumption by the producers.

Economic cooperation between the two original members was intended to overcome the developmental handicaps flowing from the small size of their internal markets. But even the combined population of 5.4 million scarcely affords a substantial mass market for industrial products, for incomes are low and are very unevenly distributed.

In 1980, Sierra Leone's aggregate GNP was US$980m., or approximately $280 *per capita*. For the same year, Liberia's GNP was estimated at $1,000m., or approximately $530 *per capita*. In both

Table 5.1 *Mano River Union: Basic Economic Data*

| Country | Population (m.) mid-1980 | Area ('000 sq. km) | Population density (inhabitants per sq. km) | Rate of population growth 1970–80 | GNP (1980) | | | | GNP per capita (av. annual growth per cent) 1960–80 | Real GDP growth (average annual growth per cent) | |
					Aggregate ($m.)	% of sub-group	% of ECOWAS	Per capita ($) 1980		1960–70	1970–80
Guinea	5.4	246	21.9	2.9	1,590	45	1	290	0.3	3.5	3.3
Liberia	1.9	111	17.1	3.4	1,000	28	1	530	1.5	5.1	1.7
Sierra Leone	3.5	72	48.6	2.6	980	27	1	280	(.)	4.3	1.6
	10.8	429			3,570	100	3	330			

(.) less than half total unit shown.
Source: World Bank (1982a,b).

countries a large proportion of the population is outside the market economy or participates only on its fringes, and *per capita* incomes in the traditional economy are far below those of the modern sector. It is reckoned that in Sierra Leone as much as 75 per cent of the population lives in rural areas in a predominantly subsistence economy that generates about one-third of the total GDP (Sierra Leone, 1974). In the case of Liberia, it is estimated that the traditional economy includes 70 per cent of the population but generates only one-fifth of the GDP (Liberia, 1977).

The monetarised sectors of the MRU economies rest on the export of primary products. In the case of Liberia, four of these – iron ore, rubber, diamonds and timber – account for 85 per cent of the value of exports, and in 1976 the export-oriented sectors generated 46 per cent of the monetary GDP and 37 per cent of the GDP as a whole. For Sierra Leone, diamonds, bauxite and a small number of agricultural products generated nine-tenths of the value of exports around the mid-1970s, representing 35 per cent of the monetary GDP and 24 per cent of the total GDP.

The activities of the modern sectors are heavily underpinned by foreign capital inflows as well as by foreign entrepreneurs and management. In 1976–7, external investment accounted for about 30 per cent of the total investment in Sierra Leone (Sierra Leone, 1977), and the share in Liberia is thought to be similar. External dependence is high not only in the enclave export sectors but also in manufacturing industries that serve the domestic markets.

Manufacturing industry itself, as distinct from artisanal production, currently plays only a minor role in the two economies, despite governmental measures to stimulate its growth during the past two decades. In Sierra Leone in 1980, manufactures generated only 5 per cent of the GDP, while in Liberia they generated about 9 per cent of the GDP. Industrial production is concentrated in Freetown and Monrovia. Its range and the relative importance of different sectors are typical of countries at this stage of economic development; it mainly consists of relatively simple import substitutes, of which each country produces largely similar types. Production includes biscuits and confectionary; beer and alcoholic beverages; tobacco products; building and construction materials; metal hollow ware; travel goods; soap and candles; garments and footwear; explosives. Production is characterised by generally high costs and, typically, the share of local value-added in production costs is relatively small. In many cases the contribution of local production to foreign exchange savings appears to be marginal or negative (UN Industrial Development Organisation, 1976). Much plant and equipment is idle, even though very similar products continue to be imported in both countries.

The newest member of the MRU, Guinea, has many geophysical, ethnic and economic similarities with its two partners, but differs from them in at least three important respects: it lacks a creole element; it is francophone; and since independence, under Sekou Touré's regime, it has espoused a rigidly socialist economy characterised by direct state control of production and consumption in every sector except mining. Private trade, discouraged since independence, had virtually ceased by 1975. Two years later, however, following widespread disturbances that culminated in demonstrations by market women, a resumption of petty trade was conceded, and in 1978 and 1979 other measures of economic liberalisation followed. Guinea's population of 5.4 million is as large as that of Liberia and Sierra Leone combined. Its GNP in 1980 was $1,590m. and GNP *per capita* amounted to $290.

Like its two partners, Guinea is well endowed with natural resources, including 30 per cent of the world's known reserves of bauxite, which generate, with alumina, the bulk of export earnings. The production of iron ore has been resumed and should become increasingly important. However, despite the rapid development of mining in recent years, traditional agriculture remains the principal economic activity in terms of employment and output (generating 43 per cent of the GDP in 1976), although its growth has been slow. The staple food crops are rice, cassava and maize. There is a substantial livestock herd. The principal commercial crops are bananas, coffee, pineapples, palm kernels, groundnuts and citrus fruits. Guinea has a small manufacturing sector in which several of the plants are relatively large in scale. They include factories for textiles, food and agricultural processing, cement, and a construction materials plant. Their economic performance has been uniformly poor. Impending developments include an oil refinery, a steelworks and a cement plant.

Detailed statistics on the structure of production and growth and on the structure of trade, growth and export in the MRU are included in Tables 6.2 and 6.3 on pp. 90 and 91.

THE OBJECTIVES, INSTITUTIONS AND POLICIES OF THE MRU

The 1973 Declaration calls for the establishment of a customs union, to be termed the Mano River Union, whose stated aims and objectives are (1) to expand trade by the elimination of all barriers to mutual trade, by the creation of conditions favourable to an expansion of mutual productive capacity, and by cooperation in the creation of new productive capacity; and (2) to secure a fair distribution of the benefits from economic cooperation. Of the protocols subsequently adopted to give effect to these broad objectives, the Twelfth, on Union industries, is by far the most important potentially for the industrial development of the MRU. It outlines arrangements for industrial cooperation, and an embryo regional policy. Union industries are those that depend on the combined market and the MRU is intended to have an important role in their promotion and location through the provision of incentives. With the aim of preventing unbalanced development, it is specifically envisaged that a Union industry might be invited to accept a location that would be suboptimal from its point of view. The Protocol prescribes that compensation should be paid to any such industry, the cost of which is to be borne equally by member states. These provisions make it clear that the Mano River Union is intended to be a good deal more than a simple customs union.

The MRU is to be established in two main phases. The first phase, which was to have been completed by 1 January 1977, involves the liberalisation of mutual trade in goods of 'local origin' through the elimination of tariff and non-tariff barriers; the harmonisation of tariff rates and of fiscal incentives for freely traded goods in order to ensure fair trading conditions; and the adoption of supporting cooperative measures for increasing the output of agricultural and manufactured products of 'local origin'. (Goods are designated as of local origin if they are wholly produced in the area or, for manufactures using imported materials, if local value-added accounts for at least 35 per cent of the ex-factory price of the finished product.) This period of Union activity was thus to be concerned mainly, in a Tinbergian sense, with measures of 'negative integration' – namely, with the establishment of the machinery of the customs union – but not entirely so, since even during these initial years cooperation in a number of other important fields – including fiscal harmonisation – was also envisaged. During the second phase, for which no timetable or plan of action is specified, the Union's economic objectives of accelerated economic growth and social progress are to be pursued by building on these foundations, by establishing Union industries and by other means, taking into account the necessity for a fair distribution of the benefits.

To bring about all these developments, a complex institutional system has been established. At its apex is the supreme policy-making and decision-taking institution of the Union, the Union Ministerial Council (UMC), which includes all ministers whose portfolios are closely involved in Union activities. Since the UMC acts on the basis of consensus, the support of two (now three) governments is needed.

Decisions are taken on the basis of draft proposals from the Standing Committee, itself composed of senior national officials, which in turn receives proposals from subcommittees. A number of 'implementing organs' have been established by protocol to carry out Union activities in training and research, industry and trade, transport and postal affairs. Of these, the Union Commission on Industry and Trade (UCIT), constituted by the Ministers of Planning, Industry, and Trade and Finance, together with the Union's Secretary-General, evidently has a key role. The 'implementing organs' are empowered to take certain executive actions – usually by consensus – but any of their recommendations that obligate the member state financially, or that require national legislation, have to be approved by the UMC before being implemented by each of the governments. The composition of the UCIT ensures, however, that it can effectively make the final decisions at Union level on all Union matters relating to industry and trade.

The function of the Secretariat is to carry on the administration of the Union under the direction of the UMC. It is responsible for the day-to-day operations of the Union, oversees its activities on a continuing basis and also prepares projects and programmes to be undertaken in the various areas of cooperation between the two countries. It is the only continuously operating organ of the Union, since the UMC, the implementing organs and other committees meet only intermittently.

Dissatisfaction with the operations and achievements of the Union's institutions prompted the UMC in 1976 to subject their structure, procedures and performance to external evaluation. The resulting report (Commonwealth Secretariat, 1978) questions the appropriateness of the structures and makes a number of recommendations (pp. 135–9) for streamlining procedures, and for rendering them more effective in terms of decision-making and as an instrument for development. The report lays considerable emphasis on the necessity for the activities of the Union to be integrated with national development plans, and for a more effective two-way process of interaction to be developed. Recommendations for improving the capacity of the Secretariat are made with this end in mind.

PROGRESS TOWARDS THE ESTABLISHMENT OF A CUSTOMS UNION

Although the MRU's present institutional arrangements clearly have their limitations, they have succeeded in effecting considerable progress towards the establishment of a customs union and the implementation of other requirements during the first phase. Harmonised customs and excise legislation, administration and procedures have been adopted and substantial progress has been made towards the establishment of a common external tariff (CET) and towards excise harmonisation. In 1977 the CET involving a common classification, valuation and statistical codes, and embodying uniform rates on 95 per cent of the tariff items on the schedules, was adopted for implementation by the respective legislatures. By January 1980, fewer than 100 of the 1,000 main customs headings remained to be harmonised, of which 45 fell within chapter 29 (Organic Chemicals). The effective tariff uniformity achieved is rather less than these figures suggest since both member states maintain certain other charges of an equivalent effect to import duties – such as fees for import licences (10 per cent) and invoice entries in Sierra Leone – thereby significantly raising the effective level of duty, apart from deharmonising aggregate import charges over the entire range of tariff headings.

A further important limitation of the customs-union arrangements is that provisions do not exist for the free circulation of third-country goods inside the MRU, or for the transfer of duty on any imports consumed in a country other than that of original importation. Their absence must limit the potential commercial benefits of the Union.

Trade liberalisation is an important part of the first stage of the Union's development, although not automatic. Before trade in any product is liberalised, three conditions had originally to be satisfied: (1) the good must be placed on the official list of goods of local origin (the decision in this respect is taken by UCIT, in accordance with the Eleventh Protocol, after application by the manufacturer); (2) it must be a product for which the external tariff rates of the member states have been harmonised; and (3) where the product is subject to excise duty in either country it must, if manufactured, be placed on the list of products for which those rates have also been harmonised. Excises are not charged on intra-Union exports, but they are payable on importation to another member state and are then retained by its Treasury. By 1980, agreement had been reached on the harmonisation of about two-thirds of excise rates, but progress on the rest proved to be difficult. It was decided at a ministerial meeting in Monrovia in January 1981 that this third requirement should no longer apply.

The removal of this obstacle was promptly followed on 1 May 1981 by the formal commencement of tariff-free trade for wholly produced goods and for those manufactured products of local origin that satisfied the other requirements. Non-tariff barriers of various kinds continue to impede intra-Union trade in liberalised products however. Overt barriers include Sierra Leone's system of import and export licencing and, at the commercial level, such constraints as restrictive distribution clauses in franchise agreements with multinational corporations, of which that affecting the export of Heineken beer is a notable example. Other official obstacles include border control procedures, documentation requirements, export duties imposed by Sierra Leone, and payments difficulties. Thus, although the main legislative and administrative procedures of the customs union have been established, much remains to be done before it becomes fully effective.

THE DEVELOPMENTAL IMPACT AND POTENTIAL OF THE MRU

A customs union is not an end in itself, but must find its economic justification in its contribution to the economic growth and development of the member states. In this regard, both static trade expansion based on the existing industrial structures, and dynamic effects accompanying the development of new industries to serve the combined MRU markets, will depend to a considerable extent on the structure and level of the tariff adopted. In terms of orthodoxy, harmonisation of rates of duty should be undertaken at levels that are appropriate as regards both revenue and protection.

The criteria used in arriving at the rates adopted in the CET of the MRU were never made fully explicit (see, however, MRU, 1976a). The principal aim was apparently to attain rate uniformity without generating significant revenue losses for either participant – an aspect specifically emphasised in a revenue symposium held prior to the formulation of the CET. Protective as distinct from revenue considerations have evidently been taken into account in the case of the relatively few products so far produced by established industries. There is no evidence that the CET rests on a systematic attempt to determine an optimal tariff policy reflecting both existing production advantages of the individual member states in various sectors and optimal patterns of growth in the middle term. Admittedly, given the present state of knowledge on levels of effective protection and domestic resource costs in the countries concerned, any such attempt could scarcely have been very solidly grounded in any case.

The orthodox emphasis on the primacy of tariff policy in African economic integration is, however, somewhat misplaced, and has been for some time. In no African country is protection provided solely by tariffs. Other forms of protection have become important, and the tariffs on final products have consequently become only one element – and not always the most important – in the whole package of incentives that influence the degree of a country's industrial development and the character of regional specialisation. This has been the case in Liberia, Sierra Leone and Guinea, and the enactments of the MRU likewise envisage that the development of Union industries is to be encouraged by income-tax exemptions and other incentives, including remissions of duty on inputs.

It is, therefore, vital for attaining the resource allocation objectives of regional groupings that there should be a measure of harmonisation of fiscal incentives, as well as of tariffs, since in isolation a common external tariff does not entail that industries compete on level terms. The MRU Declaration recognised this, and action on incentive harmonisation was to have been taken during the first phase. But although agreement has been reached on the general character of the incentives to be granted to Union industries, and certain more specific proposals have also been made for fiscal harmonisation in this and other areas (Lent, 1974; Commonwealth Secretariat, 1979), fiscal incentives remain an area of Union policy in which little concrete progress has been made. Up to a point, a selective approach in dealing with applications for national fiscal incentives is inevitable, since it is impossible to evaluate necessary or desirable levels of protection in advance of concretely formulated projects that can be subjected to careful evaluation. But without the formulation of guidelines related to objective criteria, the level of industrial protection in the MRU will remain largely a national choice, and the attainment of an appropriate pattern of specialisation, subject to the requirement of balance, may consequently be rendered unattainable. Just as importantly, the distribution of benefits between domestic and foreign interests may also be adversely affected.

Against this background, what are the prospects (1) for static trade expansion in the MRU, that is, trade based on existing capacity, and (2) for expanded industrial development to take advantage of the integrated market that would, in due course, generate new trade?

A consideration of the prospects for static trade expansion can best begin with the pre-liberalisation position when trade between Sierra Leone and Liberia was of the order of only 2 per cent of their total trade, of which a substantial part was represented by re-exports that would be unaffected by free trade. Unrecorded trade in traditional produce and smuggled manufactures might amount to a further 1 per cent. The narrow domestic industrial base and the inability of local industries to meet the specific requirements of more than a small part of existing local markets, as evidenced by the coexistence of chronic surplus capacity and large imports of very similar products, suggest that intra-Union trade could well fail to expand significantly in the short term.

Moreover, any trade expansion that takes place without the displacement of a similar domestic product in the partner country will largely represent trade diversion. This, though beneficial to the exporting country, will – in isolation – be detrimental to the interests of the importing country. Trade creation proper, involving a reduction of output in existing high-cost industries in one or other of the partner countries, is also conceivable, but seems unlikely to be enthusiastically welcomed or facilitated in individual cases, although 'balanced' trade creation should be mutually beneficial and, for specific products, some reciprocal arrangements having this effect might sensibly be negotiated. An instance is the possible willingness on the part of Liberia to sacrifice its relatively high-cost biscuit industry in return for trade benefits for its sugar refinery (Commonwealth Secretariat, 1978).

Allowing for all of these possibilities, the production impact of the Union arising from improved resource allocation in existing industries seems unlikely to be large, and any short-term income gains will be correspondingly small. The results of the initial period of trade liberalisation certainly do not support any other conclusion. In these respects, of course, the position of the MRU is by no means unique.

The limited scope for a favourable static impact from integration in MRU is not in itself a valid criticism of the basic policy, for the criterion is to an extent irrelevant. The essential case for regional integration in the MRU, as elsewhere, rests on its potential contribution to development. This arises not so much from orthodox trade expansion gains, but mainly from the potential impact on income and growth that a union makes possible through its impact on investment opportunities and through the scope afforded for rationalising the emergent structure of industrial production. The customs union provides a foundation for securing these developmental gains, if the level and structure of protection are right and other circumstances are favourable. Ultimately the case for the MRU stands or falls by its potential development impact by way of these channels. From this point of view, the provisions of Protocol 12, relating to the establishment of Union industries, are probably more important than any other part of the agreement.

A Union industry is an approved new industry or a substantial expansion of an existing one that is dependent on the combined market. Protocol 12 outlines the incentives for which such industries are eligible. They are to be regulated and encouraged by licences, by guarantees, and by Union investment incentives. The Commission is charged with determining the location of Union industries, with proposing measures to achieve industrial balance, and with overseeing prices and quantity. The Secretariat for its part has potentially important and wide-ranging responsibilities in relation to industrial evaluation and initiation.

When a Union licence is granted, no customs duties or equivalent charges will be levied on the goods manufactured by the Union industry and entering intra-Union trade. Hence, without regard to their local value-added content, the products of Union-licenced industries are automatically to be treated as goods of local origin. Specific fiscal incentives provided under the Union Investment Incentive Contract include: tariff protection for a period of six years; exemption from import duty up to 90 per cent of the dutiable value of approved imports of raw materials and semi-processed products used in the productive process; and exemption from the payment of income tax. Non-fiscal incentives include: the right to unrestricted transfer of funds within and outside the MRU for normal commercial purposes; unrestricted movement of factors of production within the Union; factory sites on industrial estates; technical assistance from the Secretariat for preparing and implementing projects; compensation for uneconomic location. In addition, a Union industry may be sheltered from domestic competition by being guaranteed the right of sole manufacture. These provisions afford an apparently generous package of incentives. Will they suffice, in conjunction with the newly integrated market, to stimulate substantial new development?

In an attempt to throw some light on this question, a 'prefeasibility' study of the prospects for Union industries was commissioned by the MRU. The resulting report (UN Industrial Development Organisation, 1976) identifies nine industries as having import-replacement possibilities: glass containers, rubber tyres, salt from seawater, detergent manufacture, agricultural implements, textile printing, synthetic textile weaving, dry-cell batteries, and sardinella fishing. In addition, four possible export-oriented Union industries were studied, namely iron and steel, alumina, paper and pulp and plywood. Eight other industries were also considered for Union industry status but rejected.

The locations recommended in the 1976 UNIDO study for the nine identified industries were chosen partly on economic factors (in particular, the availability of raw materials, existing plants and markets) and partly on the need to establish an equitable distribution of benefits. Within each country, the chosen locations were almost entirely based on the already available infrastructure in the capital cities of Freetown and Monrovia. Regional disparities within Sierra Leone and Liberia did not influence the chosen locations, although both governments have some commitment to reducing them. The proposed industry distribution was fairly even between the two countries, but if all of the recommended industries were to be established at the envisaged scales the balance of benefits in terms of domestic value-added, employment and volume of capital investment would favour Liberia.

In the light of the UNIDO report, the Union Commission on Industry and Trade subsequently selected eleven industries for consideration for Union industry status and four export industries, subject to further studies. The results of the further studies are believed to conclude that the pre-feasibility studies were overoptimistic. The fact that not a single industry had been granted Union industry status up to March 1982 makes it hard to disagree – although this may be due in some cases as much to an unwillingness on the part of the member states to reach the necessary compromises as to any basic lack of viability of the projects themselves. In short, although the establishment of the MRU should on general grounds improve the prospects for expanded industrial development to serve the home market, and although it is indisputable that the developmental impact of the Union must largely hinge on that, the studies referred to and the marked lack of progress to date raise grave doubts as to whether much can be expected in this direction in the foreseeable future.

As to the alternative of basing industrial development on exporting outside the Union – the MRU has considered a modest scheme of export incentive for manufactures – there is no evidence from recorded export performance or 'revealed' comparative advantage to suggest that this would be feasible. None of the member states is currently a significant exporter of manufactures to other West African countries, and the development of the larger West African preferential area is unlikely to improve their prospects significantly in the absence of a strong regional industrial policy. There is no reason to suppose either that, merely as a result of production economies that may be engendered by industrial cooperation, the MRU would be enabled to break into the wider world market, either for components or for final manufactures. In short, there seems little basis from any direction for expecting that the MRU itself will enable manufacturing industry to make a significant contribution towards accelerating economic development in the foreseeable future.

No doubt a number of new industries might be created from the further development of agriculture, forestry, mining and energy resources, for which Sierra Leone, Liberia and Guinea are extremely well placed. But by no means all of these opportunities would necessarily depend on the customs union or on other related forms of regional cooperation for their success. One notable exception is the integrated development of the Mano river basin, the recent proposals for which would call for a major effort of cooperation for development. The UN report of 1973 rightly emphasised the importance of natural resources as a basis for accelerated development, but so far the activities of the MRU have given little weight to these sectors.

PROBLEMS AND PROSPECTS

The structure, strategy and evolution to date of the MRU mirror features that, elsewhere in Africa, have produced largely ineffectual arrangements for cooperation and integration. In particular, there has been a familiar preoccupation with purely technical aspects of 'negative' integration and with trade liberalisation. After nine years of existence, the pretentious panoply of the Union has had little impact either on trade or on development. During the eighteen-month period following the introduction of liberalised trade (1 May 1981 – 30 November 1982), Sierra Leone exported manufactured products free of tariffs to Liberia amounting to only Le 780,000 ($610,000 at November 1982 rates), of which about two-thirds was accounted for by biscuits and sweets. During the same period, Liberia's tariff-free exports to Sierra Leone, wholly of plywood, amounted to Le 360,000. Even more disturbing is the fact that, six years after the adoption of Protocol 12, not a single industry had been approved for Union industry status. In attempting to improve its performance, MRU faces problems that arise from the inclusion of Guinea and from concurrent commitments to the Economic Community of West African States, to which all three countries belong.

In principle, the accession of Guinea ought substantially to improve the industrial potential of the MRU. It involves a doubling of the group's GNP, as well as preferential access to a more diverse range of products of local origin including, notably, livestock, and to a population with well-developed though suppressed trading instincts. Realistically it is difficult to be sanguine about the change. Immense difficulties will have to be resolved in the integration of Guinea's centrally planned socialist economy, where state-controlled corporations play a central role, with the largely private-enterprise economies of Liberia and Sierra Leone. One need only cite the experience of Tanzania's state trading corporations within the East African Community (Hazlewood, 1975) and of Congo's state plants in UDEAC for evidence of the intractability that these problems have shown in other African regional groupings.

Although an added constraint stems from the very different administrative and fiscal systems of francophone and anglophone Africa, their effect may be lessened by the need for all members of the MRU to harmonise their approaches within the much wider context of ECOWAS. Thus, fiscal and tariff harmonisation will soon have to be embarked upon by Sierra Leone, Liberia and Guinea if the requirements of ECOWAS are to be met.

The potential constraint of the ECOWAS dimension operates because of the necessity for the policies of MRU to be consistent with the obligations imposed by the wider grouping. The broad objectives and approaches of the two groupings are, of course, similar. Nevertheless, there appears until recently to have been insufficient coordination of their decisions. Despite an overlapping national membership of relevant bodies at technical and political levels, integration measures in certain fields have sometimes been adopted by one organisation without taking proper account of existing or projected measures in the same fields in the other. The technical issue of the tariff nomenclatures adopted by ECOWAS and MRU is a case in point: they are similar but not identical. Again, the rules of origin of the two groupings are not identical. Most important of all, it seems unlikely that the industrial privileges envisaged for Union industries could all be regarded as compatible with the 1975 Lagos Treaty. Such differences may ultimately constitute an obstacle to the easy coexistence of the two groups.

A still more important question in this context is whether there can be a continuing role for MRU if ECOWAS begins to prosper. The former could presumably continue to serve a useful purpose if it could bring about a more intimate form of integration amongst its three members than would be feasible in the foreseeable future through ECOWAS. To do this would require that Sierra Leone, Liberia and Guinea be granted waivers from compliance with various provisions of the Lagos Treaty and subsequent decisions. The MRU is already in breach of Article 20, and it is probable that the implementation of Protocol 12 would make matters worse. It would be difficult, however, without opening the floodgates, for ECOWAS to accept a case for the necessary waivers or derogations except perhaps for those countries that fall into the least developed category of membership.

Clearly, the MRU confronts a dilemma. It needs 'to deliver' to justify its continued existence, and it is undesirable in any case that it should 'mark time' during the problematic progress of ECOWAS. At the same time, it must have in mind the potential impact that the trade liberalisation of that larger economic community will have for its own activities. This will mean, notably, that any programmes for the development of Union industries will have to be elaborated with an eye to their viability in a wider preferential arrangement.

Reality now needs to be given to MRU cooperation by reaching the compromises necessary for establishing Union industries and utilising idle capacity, and by reaching agreement on the joint development of agricultural and other natural resources on which any substantial agro-industrial growth prospects are likely to hinge. It remains to be seen whether Sierra Leone, Liberia and Guinea – all of which domestically confront pressing economic and political problems – have the will to do this.

6 The Economic Community of West African States (ECOWAS)

THE BACKGROUND TO THE FORMATION OF ECOWAS

The original conception of a West African economic community (WAEC) that would include all the countries of the region goes back to 1963 (Onitiri, 1963; Adedeji, 1976), but the initiatives and negotiations that led directly to the formation of ECOWAS began only after the end of the Nigerian civil war. Nigeria played the leading role in these later moves and for three years she waged an intensive campaign to bring the community into existence (Ojo, 1980).

Nigeria's desire to foster a broader West African community has grown out of several factors. Initially a broader community was seen as an important instrument for reducing the dependence of the region on Western Europe and the USA. At the same time it was prompted by Nigeria's determination to consolidate and develop its own political and economic leadership in the region. In that context it was seen more specifically as a means of reducing the influence of France in the francophone African states, which was perceived to be harmful to Nigeria's interests. Two of the many instances that rankled were the wartime recognition of Biafra by Ivory Coast and the prospective formation of the purely francophone CEAO itself. Later a West African economic community was also perceived to be a useful vehicle for advancing Nigeria's long-term aim of finding an alternative to its increasingly oil-dependent economic strategy, its political leaders having in the end concluded that, despite Nigeria's economic weight, this would be more easily achieved through economic cooperation with its neighbours than alone.

Once the Nigerian leadership had become convinced that the interests of the state lay in the establishment of a WAEC, its problem was to persuade its prospective partners that their interests would also be served by its formation. For some of them, more particularly most of the francophone countries, that did not appear to be self-evident. They were concerned with the possibility of Nigerian domination and with the conceivably adverse implications that their adherence might have for their aid receipts from France. The pre-emptive formation of the alternative grouping of CEAO and differences of language and culture reinforced the difficulties. In its attempts to overcome them, Nigeria's strategy was to seek to isolate her immediate neighbours (Benin and Niger) from the other francophone countries, with the help of Togo, with which very cordial relations had been maintained since 1962, and to use the support of those countries to persuade others to support the wider grouping. The provision of extensive economic aid to Togo and Benin served to reassure them and to emphasise the potential benefits of cooperation with Nigeria to other waiverers.

At first Nigeria's efforts made little headway. Whatever the merits of its contention that a wider economic community would be a more effectual developmental instrument that could serve the interests of all prospective participants, the political climate in the region, and in particular the lack of trust among certain of its leaders, were powerful obstacles to its acceptance. Although the anglophone countries, together with Guinea, Benin and Togo, displayed a willingness to cooperate in the setting-up of a broader community, four of CEAO's six members – Senegal, Ivory Coast, Upper Volta and Mali – continued to oppose its formation. In the end, however, Nigerian diplomacy prevailed. For this, the fortuitous impact of the negotiations between the European Economic Community and the associable African, Caribbean and Pacific states over the replacement for the Yaoundé Convention may partly have been responsible. The constructive role played by Nigeria in those negotiations appears to have allayed some of the fears of her smaller neighbours and to have established a confidence in Nigeria's bona fides. The favourable outcome of the negotiations also seemed to confirm the fruitfulness of African cooperation for international bargaining purposes. The weight of General Gowon's personal diplomacy also told, as did the persuasive advocacy of Adebayo Adedeji, the Nigerian Commissioner for Economic Development and a principal architect of ECOWAS. The resulting improvement in the political climate helped to make discussions on an alternative community possible, and ultimately fruitful.

Already, in 1972, a Nigeria–Togo Commission had been established to work out the details of a WAEC. Undeterred by the signing of the CEAO Treaty in April 1973, a joint Nigeria–Togo ministerial delegation shortly afterwards embarked on an intensive exercise in shuttle diplomacy in an effort to bring the wider economic community into being. Every West African country except Guinea–Bissau was visited to urge a ministerial-level conference to discuss the Commission's own proposals for the broader community. That conference took place in Lomé in the following December, at which the Nigeria–Togo proposals were adopted. There followed in May 1975 the Lagos summit of heads of state and government, which adopted the draft treaty arising from the Lomé proposals. By December, all fifteen signatories had ratified the Treaty, and Cape Verde adhered soon after.

THE ECONOMIC SETTING OF WESTERN AFRICAN INTEGRATION

The Economic Community of West African States that grew out of this complex background brings together sixteen countries covering an area of 6m. sq.km that stretches from Mauretania in the north-west to Nigeria in the south-east. The Cape Verde Islands also form a part of the Community. Of its member states, five are officially anglophone, eight francophone, two lusophone and for one the official language is arabic. All of its member states are principally primary producers, who depend on a small number of agricultural and mineral products for the bulk of their incomes, employment and export earnings.

The Community's total population is almost 150 million, but most member states have very small populations. Three countries have populations of less than 1 million and no fewer than eight do not exceed 5 million. Only two member states – Ghana and Nigeria – have populations in excess of 10 million and, at 85 million, the population of the latter represents nearly 60 per cent of the combined population.

Per capita incomes are generally low. The average GNP was about $760 *per capita* in 1980, including subsistence incomes, but this figure is greatly influenced by Nigeria's large population and high income level. Generally low incomes, an uneven distribution of income and the large area of the majority of the separate national markets render the effective market size even more limited for purposes of industrialisation.

The region's economic development during the modern period has depended heavily on the advanced industrialised countries for trade, capital, technology and skills, and this dependence is still very marked. The bulk of the Community's foreign trade continues to be transacted with the advanced industrialised countries of Western Europe, but more recently the United States and Japan have constituted increasingly important markets.

Table 6.1   ECOWAS: Population, Income and Growth

Country	Population (m.) 1980	Area ('000 sq.km)	Population density (inhabitants per sq.km)	Rate of population growth 1970–80	GNP (1980) Aggregate ($m.)	% of sub-group	% of ECOWAS	Per capita ($) 1980	GNP per capita (real av. annual growth per cent) 1960–80	Real GDP growth (average annual growth per cent) 1960–70	1970–80
CEAO											
Ivory Coast	8.3	322	25.8	5.0	9,550	56	8	1,150	2.5	8.0	6.7[a]
Upper Volta	6.1	274	22.3	1.8	1,280	7	1	210	0.1	3.0	3.5
Mali	7.0	1,240	5.6	2.7	1,340	8	1	190	1.4	3.3	4.9
Mauretania	1.5	1,031	1.6	2.5	660[b]	4	1	440[b]	1.6[b]	..	1.7
Niger	5.3	1,267	4.2	2.8	1,760	10	2	330	−1.6	2.9	2.7
Senegal	5.7	196	29.1	2.8	2,560	15	2	450	−0.3	2.5	2.5[a]
	33.9	4.330			17,150	100	15	510			
Mano River Union											
Guinea	5.4	246	21.9	2.9	1,590	45	1	290	0.3	3.5	3.3
Liberia	1.9	111	17.1	3.4	1,000	28	1	530	1.5	5.1	1.7
Sierra Leone	3.5	72	48.6	2.6	980	27	1	280	(.)	4.3	1.6
	10.8	429			3,570	100	3	330			
Other ECOWAS countries											
Benin	3.4	113	30.1	2.6	1,050		1	310	0.4	2.6	3.3
Ghana	11.7	239	49.0	3.0	4,920		4	420	−1.0	2.1	−0.1
Nigeria	84.7	924	91.7	2.5	85,510		75	1,010	4.1	3.1	6.5
Togo	2.5	57	43.9	2.5	1,020		1	410	3.0	8.5	3.4
Guinea–Bissau	0.8	36	22.2	..	130		(.)	160	..	..	..
The Gambia	0.6	11	54.5	3.1[a]	150		(.)	250	1.7	..	..
Cape Verde	0.3	4	75.0	2.0[a]	100		(.)	300	..	..	..
Total ECOWAS	148.7	6,143			113,600		100	760			

[a] 1970–9.
[b] The estimates of GNP and growth rate for Mauretania should be treated with reserve. Alternative World Bank estimates (e.g. *Atlas*) suggest a substantially lower GNP ($530m.) and a negative annual growth rate (−0.7%).
.. not available.

Table 6.2   ECOWAS: Structure of Production and Growth

Distribution of GDP (%) and growth rates (annual averages)

Country	Agriculture				Industry				Manufacturing				Services			
	% share 1960	Rate of growth 1960–70	% share 1980	Rate of growth 1970–80	% share 1960	Rate of growth 1960–70	% share 1980	Rate of growth 1970–80	% share 1960	Rate of growth 1960–70	% share 1980	Rate of growth 1970–80	% share 1960	Rate of growth 1960–70	% share 1980	Rate of growth 1970–80
CEAO																
Ivory Coast	43	4.2	34[b]	3.4[a]	14	11.5	22[b]	10.5[a]	7	11.6	11[b]	7.2[a]	43	9.7	44[b]	7.0[a]
Upper Volta	62	..	40	1.2	14	..	18	3.2	8	..	13	3.7	24	..	42	5.7
Mali	55	..	42	4.4	10	..	10	3.0	5	..	6	..	35	..	48	6.0
Mauretania	59	..	26	−1.1	24	..	33	(.)	3	..	8	0.2	17	..	41	6.8
Niger	69	3.3	33	−3.7	9	13.9	34	11.3	4	..	8	..	22	(.)	33	6.9
Senegal	24	2.9	29[b]	3.7[a]	17	4.4	24[b]	3.7[a]	12	6.2	19[b]	3.8[a]	59	1.7	47[b]	1.5[a]
Mano River Union																
Guinea	..	..	37	..	..	..	33	..	..	..	4	..	..	..	30	..
Liberia	..	..	36	4.7	..	..	31	−0.2	..	..	9	8.0	..	..	33	1.9
Sierra Leone	..	..	36	2.2	..	..	20	−3.8	..	..	5	3.8	..	..	44	4.2
Other ECOWAS Countries[c]																
Benin	55	..	43	..	8	..	12	..	3	..	7	..	37	..	45	..
Ghana	..	−0.4	66	−1.2	..	..	21	−1.2	..	..	..	−2.9	..	..	13	1.0
Nigeria	63	..	20	0.8	11	12.0	42	8.1	5	9.1	6	12.0	26	4.9	38	9.7
Togo	55	..	26	0.8	16	..	20	6.6	8	..	7	..	29	..	54	3.9

[a] 1970–9.
[b] 1979.
[c] Data for The Gambia, Guinea–Bissau and Cape Verde not available.
.. not available.
(.) less than half total unit shown.
Source: World Bank (1982b), Annex, *World Development Indicators.*

Table 6.3 ECOWAS: Trade, Growth and Export Structure

Country	Merchandise trade ($m.) Exports 1980	Imports 1980	Average annual growth rate (%) Exports 1960–70	Exports 1970–80	Imports 1960–70	Imports 1970–80	Terms of trade (1975 = 100) 1960	1980	% share of merchandise exports — Fuels, minerals, metals 1960	1979	Other primary commodities 1960	1979	Textiles and clothing 1960	1979	Machinery and transport equipment 1960	1979	Other manufactures 1960	1979	Value of manufactured exports ($m.) 1962	1979
CEAO																				
Ivory Coast	2,700	2,650	8.8	4.6	9.7	8.1	113	102	1	5	98	87	—	2	(.)	2	1	4	2	212
Upper Volta	45	330	15.9	2.0	7.7	7.9	88	89	—	1	100	87	—	3	(.)	3	(.)	6	1	10
Mali	200	290	3.0	9.4	-0.4	3.4	107	91	—	(.)a	96b	99a	1b	(.)	1b	(.)	2b	1a	(-)	2a
Mauretania	194	255	50.7	-1.1	4.5	5.6	149	77	4b	89	69b	11	1b	(.)	20b	(.)a	6b	(.)a	2	4a
Niger	290	630	6.0	12.8	11.9	15.8	98	80	..	40a	100	25a	—	1a	—	—a	—	34a	1	76a
Senegal	520	1,200	1.2	1.2	2.3	4.1	71	63	3	29	94	63	1	1	1	1	1	6	5	41
Mano River Union																				
Guinea	421	375	..	..	..	..	..	..	42	98a	58	2a	—	—	—	(.)	—	—	..	55a
Liberia	601	640	18.4	1.0	2.9	1.2	255	71	45	39	55	35	—	(.)	—	1	—	25	3	139
Sierra Leone	240	420	0.3	-4.8	1.9	-3.0	111	84	15	8a	20	48a	—	—	—	—	65	44a	23c	72a
Other ECOWAS countries d																				
Benin	54	360	5.0	-7.6	7.4	4.8	114	82	10	2a	80	90a	7	3a	(.)	2a	3	3a	1	2a
Ghana	960	900	0.2	-8.4	-1.5	-3.3	111	110	7	16a	83	83a	—	(.)	—	(.)	10	1a	12	12a
Nigeria	26,000	15,000	6.6	2.6	1.6	1.6	39	173	8	91a	89	8a	—	(.)	—	(.)	3	1a	34	148a
Togo	640	630	10.5	1.6	8.6	12.4	56	74	3	62a	89	31a	3	3a	—	3a	5	1a	1	17a

a 1978.
b 1961.
c 1963.
d Data for The Gambia, Guinea–Bissau and Cape Verde not available.
.. not available.
(.) less than half total unit shown.
Source: World Bank (1982b), Annex, World Development Indicators.

THE LEVEL AND STRUCTURE OF INTRA-COMMUNITY TRADE

By comparison with total external trade, intra-Community trade is relatively unimportant. For the years 1974, 1976 and 1978, the values of recorded intra-Community exports at current prices were $409m., $478m. and $616m. respectively, representing 3–3.5 per cent of total exports (UN Conference on Trade and Development, 1981). Even if unrecorded trade is allowed for, which is quite significant for several states (UN Economic Commission for Africa, 1978), intra-Community trade is unlikely to have exceeded 5–6 per cent of total trade.

A more detailed view of intra-Community trade must be based at present on data for 1975. The incomplete and unreliable nature of the trade data even for that year is underlined by a value of recorded intra-Community exports that is 20 per cent higher than that for imports.

In 1975, the countries that accounted for the bulk of intra-Community trade were Ivory Coast and Nigeria (one-third each) and Senegal (one-sixth). The land-locked countries together with Benin and Ghana accounted for most of the balance. The land-locked countries appear to depend relatively more on intra-Community trade than do its other members, but the difficulty of ascertaining the true origin and destination of their trade almost certainly results in an overstatement of that dependence.

Considerable imbalances of trade are recorded in intra-ECOWAS trade. In 1975, four countries – Nigeria, Ivory Coast, Senegal and Niger – recorded positive balances, while the remaining twelve were all in deficit to varying extents. The overall position is, however, considerably affected by trade in crude oil, which accounts for most of Nigeria's favourable intra-Community balance and a large proportion of intra-Community deficits and surpluses. In manufactures, only Ivory Coast and Senegal consistently record positive trade balances.

Perhaps the most striking feature of intra-ECOWAS trade is the dominant role of intra-CEAO trade. Intra-CEAO exports as a proportion of total intra-ECOWAS exports amounted to one-half in 1975, and if trade in petroleum products is excluded this share would rise to about two-thirds, of which Ivory Coast accounts for one-half and Senegal one-quarter.

The low level of intra-Community trade is clearly produced in part by high tariffs and quantitative import restrictions. Other obstacles include exchange controls and payments difficulties, which, in varying degrees, affect trade flows in most West African countries except Liberia. A transportation system that is still geared to trade with

Europe rather than to intra-West African trade constitutes an additional constraint. But perhaps as important as any of these factors is the fact that the level of industrialisation in the Community is generally low, and that the member states in general produce a fairly limited but similar range of manufactures that cannot satisfy their own domestic requirements, let alone compete in the markets of other member states with superior and often cheaper foreign products. In 1980 the share of GDP derived from manufacturing production exceeded 15 per cent only in Senegal, and in only one other country, Ivory Coast, did it exceed 10 per cent.

The principal industries of the Community that are found in most member states are: food, drink and tobacco; textiles and garments; footwear; motor vehicle assembly; and certain chemical products such as paints, matches and plastics. In contrast, heavy manufacturing industries and industries employing advanced technologies are represented to a very limited extent.

A further significant feature of the Community from the standpoint of integration is the marked disparities in the levels of economic development of the member states and their individual importance in the economy of the Community. Nigeria's overwhelming economic preponderance places it in a category of its own. In 1980 it accounted for no less than 75 per cent of the group's GNP, 55–60 per cent of its population, 75 per cent of exports, including oil, and 55 per cent of its manufacturing industry. Other middle-income countries (that is, those with a *per capita* income of more than $410) are Ghana, Ivory Coast, Senegal, Liberia and Mauretania. Together this group accounts for about 20 per cent of the aggregate population of ECOWAS, 15 per cent of its GNP, and 37 per cent of its manufacturing industry.The remaining eleven member states all fall into the low-income category, having *per capita* incomes ranging from $190 to $410. Although they make up nearly a quarter of the Community's total population, they accounted for only 8 per cent of its GDP, 9 per cent of its manufacturing and 6 per cent of exports.

Such a dominating economic position of a single state is without parallel in other economic groupings – not excluding COMECON. Nigeria's dominance is so great that its influence on the future development of ECOWAS is bound to be decisive. The corollary is that, from its point of view, the Community offers the prospect of only a modest increase in market size and economic benefits. For the other member states by contrast, the Nigerian presence could hold out the prospect of a massive increase in the potential size of their markets. Particularly for the other middle-income countries, access to the Nigerian market could offer greatly improved industrialisation prospects if they are competitive and can meet the Community's stringent rules of origin – and this could be so even with a relatively low level of market penetration.

THE ECONOMIES OF THE ECOWAS MEMBER STATES NOT FORMING PART OF EXISTING SUB-REGIONAL GROUPINGS

With the exception of Ghana, Nigeria, Togo, Benin, Guinea, Guinea–Bissau, The Gambia and Cape Verde, all member states of ECOWAS were, at its inception, part of other West African groupings. The Gambia subsequently became involved in a Senegambian Confederation whose implications are discussed in Chapter 7, while Guinea has since joined the Mano River Union. This section is devoted to a brief outline of the salient economic characteristics of the principal member states whose economies are not elsewhere discussed, namely, Nigeria, Ghana, Benin and Togo. Together these four countries account for more than four-fifths of the Community's aggregate GDP, of which Nigeria alone accounts for three-quarters. Summary data on the growth, development and structure of the remaining member states (Guinea–Bissau and Cape Verde) are included in Tables 6.1 and 6.5.

Nigeria

Agriculture was, until quite recently, the most important sector of the Nigerian economy. During the 1960s the centre of gravity of the economy began to shift, and since the end of the civil war agriculture has been completely overtaken by the petroleum industry as the main engine of growth. Whereas in 1962 agriculture contributed 60 per cent of GDP at factor cost, by 1978–9 its contribution had declined to less than 20 per cent. Nevertheless the agricultural sector continues to be of crucial importance to the economy in providing employment for over half of Nigeria's total workforce, food to meet the needs of an expanding population, and raw materials for the expanding industrial sector.

Agricultural products constituted about four-fifths of the value of total exports in 1960. By 1970, however, their value had dropped to 44 per cent and by 1978–9 they accounted for only 6–7 per cent of the total. This relative decline is mainly due to the spectacular growth of crude petroleum exports, but it also reflects the poor performance of the agricultural sector resulting from drought, low producer prices and other factors. The main export commodities in the commercial sector are cocoa, groundnuts and groundnut oil, palm kernels, rubber, cotton and cottonseed, palm oil and timber. The output of most of these crops has declined or stagnated. Subsistence production, normally carried on side by side with production of crops for local and export use, cannot be accurately estimated. Growing points of the agricultural sector are increasingly represented by plantations and farm settlements, but the sector as a whole is in serious difficulties as is evidenced by a dramatic decline in the principal export crops and a soaring food import bill.

The share of mining in GDP has risen rapidly during the past decade. Crude petroleum is now the country's principal export earner (contributing over 90 per cent of the total). Proven reserves could last twenty years at pre-1980 extraction rates. Since 1965, part of the crude oil production has been refined at Port Harcourt, and other refineries exist at Warri and Kaduna. Natural gas, coal and a variety of other minerals, most notably tin, are found.

Both manufacturing and the construction industry grew rapidly in Nigeria from the 1950s until 1979, when their combined contribution to GDP was just over 10 per cent. Subsequently the performance of this sector has been severely affected by import restrictions. The manufacturing sector continues to be dominated by light import-substitution industries, but more emphasis is being placed on the development of consumer durables such as motor vehicles, and on capital goods and heavy industries such as iron and steel and petrochemicals.

Of Nigeria's manufacturing industries, the textile sector is the most important, but rubber, brewing, aluminium and tin products, cigarettes, extruded plastics, paper board, wire ropes, fertilisers, refrigerators, air conditioning machinery, bicycle assembly and cement are also important. Car and lorry assembly plants are in production. Nigeria's steel requirements are expected to reach 6 million tons by 1990 and an iron and steel industry is being set up to meet these needs. Plants for liquefaction of natural gas and for the manufacture of nitrogenous fertiliser are to be built.

In its attempts to develop import substitution industries for domestic and ultimately sub-regional markets and to transform Nigeria from a nation of traders to one of industrialists, the Nigerian government has adopted stringent measures for exchange control, high tariffs, import prohibitions on a wide range of consumer goods, and a strict indigenisation policy. So far, the impact of these measures has principally been to reduce efficiency by eliminating competition. Nigeria's economy continues to be largely characterised by what is sometimes termed 'commercial', as distinct from 'industrial', capitalism.

Benin

Like Senegal, but for different reasons, the small, densely populated country of Benin suffered severely from the break-up of the French West African federation (AOF). It had become accustomed to export educated manpower to the other member states, but after the break-up most were expelled. Benin is one of the poorer countries of West Africa. Its annual rate of growth of production in the past two decades has been little higher than the rate of population growth. Over the whole period GDP *per capita* increased by only 0.4 per cent per annum.

The economy is heavily dependent on the agricultural sector. The main food crops are maize, cassava, sorghum, yams, beans and millet. Cereal production is estimated to meet only 60 per cent of domestic requirements, and food supply is supplemented by fishing and livestock farming. An agricultural reform programme was launched in 1976, aimed at creating a network of socialist cooperatives. The major cash crop is still the palm. Originally based on natural groves and still largely so, the industry has in recent years also developed in part on the basis of industrial plantations. Cotton production, initially promising, has encountered problems on account of poor marketing arrangements and low publicly set producer prices, which has encouraged smuggling. Other cash crops include groundnuts and coffee.

Industrial production is still on the whole small scale and, apart from the construction material industry, it is mainly concerned with the processing of primary products for export and the production of substitutes for the simpler forms of imported consumer goods. The industrial sector increased its share of GDP from 6 per cent in 1965–6 to 15 per cent in 1976. In 1975 the country's most important industrial plant began production, namely, the textile complex at Parakou that is aimed largely at the export market. Two more textile complexes are currently planned, together with a cement plant at Porto Novo and a sugar complex in Save – in both of which Nigeria is participating – and a petroleum refinery. Since 1972, state participation in industry has increased considerably. Several private enterprises have been nationalised and most major undertakings are now government controlled.

An offshore oil field is being developed from which gains can be expected, and iron and phosphates have been located. Limestone is exploited and supplies a cement factory.

Togo

During the postwar period prior to independence, Togo's income grew relatively rapidly and this was accompanied by a rise in the rate of population growth and in urbanisation. Although the GDP growth rate for the decade 1970–80 (3.4 per cent) was less than half that recorded during the previous decade, over the two decades as a whole *per capita* incomes have increased at an average rate of 3 per cent, which compares favourably with those experienced by other African countries at similar levels of development. The main stimulus to Togo's overall economic growth during this period has come from phosphate mining. Phosphates were discovered in 1952 and exports began in 1961.

The economy nevertheless remains heavily dependent on agriculture, which provides a livelihood for 70 per cent of the population and which even in 1980 accounted for 26 per cent of GDP and 30 per cent of export earnings. The most important food crops are cassava, yams, millet, sorghums and maize. Fishing and livestock supplement the food supply. The principal export crop is cocoa, but coffee, palm kernels, groundnuts and cotton are also important crops. On the whole, in recent years, production in the cash crop sector has either stagnated or declined.

Togo's manufacturing industry is small scale and relatively little developed, but it has shown considerable growth in recent years. Production centres on the processing of agricultural commodities (palm oil extracting, coffee roasting, cassava flour milling and cotton ginning) and the import substitution of consumer goods – textiles, footwear, beverages, confectionery and tyres. Recent projects include a fertiliser factory, a petroleum refinery, a steelworks, a textile factory and a large cement plant.

Mineral products have assumed a growing importance in the economy and in 1979 they generated abut 60 per cent of export earnings. Apart from phosphates, limestone reserves are extensive and are utilised to produce clinker in the cement plant. Both Ivory Coast and Ghana participate in this venture, together with foreign interests.

Ghana

At the time of independence, Ghana's abundant land, rich mineral resources and well-educated labour force appeared to promise bright economic prospects. During the past two decades however, its performance has been amongst the worst in sub-Saharan Africa. Gross domestic product has grown only slowly and the annual average rate of growth of real *per capita* national income has been – 1.0 per cent. Inflation during the past decade has been higher than that of any other African country and – at an annual average rate of 35 per cent –

attains Latin American dimensions. Deep-seated structural problems lie at the root of this depressing economic record. They hinge on the performance and management of the large public sector and widespread distortions in the price mechanism.

Government, which employs more than 300,000 civil servants and in addition operates more than 100 parastatal organisations covering a wide range of key economic sectors, occupies a prominent place in the economy. Losses in almost all state activities have brought many state organisations to the brink of collapse and have debilitated the rest of the economy through the supply bottlenecks that have resulted. Inflation has been fuelled by such shortages, as well as by rapid increases in the money supply associated with the financing of budget deficits that have attained 40 per cent of total expenditure. The exchange rate has been greatly overvalued.

Throughout the economy the price structure has been inappropriate. In the primary producing sector for instance, prices for cocoa farmers have been extremely low. For a time, farmers were paid only one-tenth of the foreign exchange value of their cocoa by the Cocoa Marketing Board. A high proportion of the crop has been smuggled to markets in Ivory Coast, resulting in losses to the government of valuable foreign exchange and tax revenues. The latest economic recovery programme outlined in March 1982 sets out measures to rehabilitate traditional exports, reduce imports of food and curtail the budget deficit.

Despite the obstacles, agriculture and forestry nevertheless contribute two-thirds of GDP, provide employment for more than half of the workforce and generate the bulk of foreign exchange. But despite the advantages of climate, good soil and adequate water, only 10–15 per cent of suitable land is under cultivation and yields are low. The country is not self-sufficient in food crops. The principal commercial activity, cocoa, still accounts for over 50 per cent of total export earnings, despite a halving of output during the past decade. Recent measures to boost production include a tripling of producer prices. Following the New Deal for Agriculture initiated in 1980 and aimed at bringing about self-sufficiency in food, the output of food crops did rise significantly. The output of forestry continues to be adversely affected by shortages of foreign exchange and a deterioration of roads and infrastructure, and its contribution to foreign exchange has been falling.

The manufacturing sector, whose contribution to GDP is around one-fifth, is principally the outcome of the industrialisation drive of the first post-independence decade and it grew rapidly in the 1960s. The sector consists of many small firms and a few larger enterprises employing capital-intensive techniques. Production is essentially for the home market and reflects the emphasis on import substitution in the early development plans. A few plants produce primarily for export, including an aluminium smelter, timber mills and cocoa-processing plants. By African standards a relatively wide range of products is produced, but the sector is not internally integrated and a high proportion of its requirements of raw materials, semi-finished goods and spare parts have to be imported. The chronic shortage of foreign exchange largely accounts for a situation in which many enterprises operate at less than 30 per cent of capacity and overall capacity utilisation is not more than 60 per cent. In an attempt to improve the sector's performance and industrial investment, the conditions for foreign participation in a number of sectors were liberalised in the 1981 Investment Code.

The country is rich in minerals. Gold constitutes the second most important source of foreign exchange and other minerals produced for export include bauxite and manganese. The exploitation of manganese deposits has been stimulated by a recently completed processing plant. Oil is produced on a small scale from an offshore field and further exploration is under way.

Ghana's economy has much potential, but inappropriate public policies have obstructed economic growth. Widespread rehabilitation measures in agriculture, industry and infrastructure will be required before development can be resumed and Ghana is able to make its full contribution to West African integration. To carry these out will call for substantial injections of foreign aid.

THE OBJECTIVES, PROCEDURES AND INSTITUTIONS OF ECOWAS

The general objective of the Community is to promote economic development by establishing a common market and harmonising a variety of economic policies, including agricultural policies, industrial development plans and incentives, and monetary policies. There is also to be cooperation for the development of energy and mineral resources and for the joint development of infrastructure.

An important Community instrument for positive integration is its Fund for Co-operation, Compensation and Development. The Fund is not only charged with functions that are designed to promote the general development of the Community, but it is also assigned responsibilities in regional development and towards the less developed member states. The Fund is at present the most concrete manifestation of the Community's concern with promoting a fair and equitable distribution of the benefits of economic cooperation and with eliminating disparities in the levels of development of its member states, in so far as they depend on finance.

The Fund's specific purposes are: to finance projects in member states; to provide compensation to member states that have suffered losses as a result of the location of Community enterprises; to provide compensation and other forms of assistance to member states that have suffered losses arising out of the application of the provisions of the Treaty on the liberalisation of trade within the Community; to guarantee foreign investments made in member states in respect of enterprises established under the provisions of the Treaty on the harmonisation of industrial policies; to provide means to facilitate the mobilisation of internal and external financial resources for the member states and the Community; and to promote development projects in the less developed member states of the Community.

The ordinary resources of the Fund are made up, first, of the capital and annual budgetary contributions of the member states. These are assessed on the basis of a coefficient that takes account both of the country's share of the Community's aggregate GDP and its relative *per capita* income. The Fund's nominal capital was fixed at US$500m. Other envisaged resources include: foreign aid; income from loans made from the sources previously mentioned and from guarantees given by the Fund; borrowing by the Fund. The Fund has its own managing director.

A priority concern of the Treaty of Lagos is with the establishment of a customs union. A timetable is laid down for those aspects of the Community's operations that are concerned with trade liberalisation, the customs union and closely related matters. The customs union itself, involving the elimination of all tariff and non-tariff barriers on goods of Community origin, is to be established by three stages in the course of a fifteen-year period from the entry into force of the Treaty: (1) the first stage is constituted by a two-year standstill period for tariffs that terminated in May 1981; (2) the second stage comprises the next eight years over which member states must reduce and ultimately eliminate their import duties on intra-Community trade; (3) the third stage covers the five succeeding years over which the common external tariff is to be established.

Related timetabled provisions require the elimination of internal indirect taxes that discriminate against imports from member states within one year of the end of the standstill period, and the elimination of discriminatory revenue duties within eight years. Quantitative restrictions on Community goods are also to be eliminated within ten years of the entry into force of the Treaty.

The Treaty does not set out a timetable for the implementation of the other measures that will be required for the Community's progress from a customs union to a common market, and towards a true economic community. Indeed, the modalities by which the customs union itself is to be arrived at are not – unlike the case of the Treaty of Rome – specified. This and other instances of vagueness are claimed by Ojo (1980) to have been a deliberate tactic, in accord with the initial Nigeria–Togo agreement to adopt a flexible and pragmatic approach to integration and to deal only with specific issues calling for immediate attention. The alternative, claims Ojo (p. 601), probably correctly, would have been no treaty at all. The outcome is a treaty that represents a framework within which agreement can subsequently be reached on the most important issues, rather than embodying substantive agreement on most matters. The character of the customs union and the Community's industrial development and nearly all the measures for giving effect to the more positive aspects of the Community's integration remain to be worked out, agreed and embodied in further protocols and decisions.

At the institutional level, the machinery for carrying on the Community's activities is broadly similar to that found in other African integration groupings. The Community's supreme decision-making organ is the Authority of Heads of State and Government, which meets annually and whose directions and decisions are binding on all institutions of the Community and on its member states. The Authority is assisted by the Council of Ministers, which consists of two representatives of each member state.

The Council of Ministers usually meets twice a year, one of its meetings immediately preceding the annual meeting of the Authority. Its principal responsibility is to direct the operations and development of the Community and to make policy recommendations to the Authority. Its decisions must be taken unanimously. If a member state should record an objection to a proposal, the matter is referred to the Authority for final resolution. The decisions and recommendations of the Council itself are taken in the light of proposals formulated by specialist commissions, of which there are currently four: the Trade, Customs, Immigration, Monetary and Payments Commission; the Industry, Agriculture and Natural Resources Commission; the Transport, Telecommunications and Natural Resources Commission; and the Social and Cultural Affairs Commission. A Tribunal to settle disputes on the interpretation or application of the Treaty is also provided for.

As for the day-to-day administration of the Community, this is in the hands of the Executive Secretariat, which is responsible for the administration of the Community and its institutions, and for implementing decisions of the Authority and the Council. The Secretariat can itself take initiatives and propose policies and actions to the

Council of Ministers. Certain difficulties were initially encountered over the operational modes of the Fund and its relationship to the executive institutions of the Community, in particular the Secretariat. Formally, these difficulties have been resolved in an Authority decision (A/DEC 13/5/79) that declares the Fund to be an institution of the Community, in relation to which the Executive Secretary has a defined responsibility.

THE STRUCTURE OF PROTECTION, DOMESTIC RESOURCE COSTS AND COMPARATIVE ADVANTAGE IN ECOWAS

If ECOWAS is to bring about appropriate patterns of regional specialisation and trade, in particular for manufacturing activities, account will have to be taken of the comparative costs of the different member states. As noted in Chapter 3, for determining relative costs in relation to major new investments, perhaps involving Community enterprises, there is no substitute for specific social cost–benefit analyses using established techniques. To arrive at a prognosis at the level of whole industrial sectors, however, such highly specific appraisals cannot be employed, and more general indicative approaches have to be relied on.

One of the most useful of these rests on the concept of the effective rate of protection (ERP) and the related concept of domestic resource costs (DRC) which incorporates adjustments for shadow prices. A comparative study of four ECOWAS countries – Ghana, Ivory Coast, Senegal and Mali – using the latter approach was undertaken for 1972 by the World Bank (1975, 1976, 1977a, b). Its results have been used by Balassa (1978) to illuminate the structure of static comparative advantage. For this purpose, domestic resource cost coefficients are equated with 'real costs of production'.

Table 6.4, reproduced from Balassa's paper, depicts real cost in this sense for nine manufacturing sectors in Ghana, Ivory Coast, Mali and Senegal for 1972, namely: food products; textiles and clothing; footwear; wood and paper; chemical products; non-metallic mineral products; metal products (two sectors distinguished); and vehicles and transport material. Adjustments have been made to take account of costs linked to the utilisation of foreign capital and manpower, and these are reflected in the two alternative bases on which the results are shown, namely, including and excluding the excess profits of foreign enterprises – that is, those that exceed the minimum level assumed to be necessary to attract foreign capital to the country in question.

The estimates suggest that, on average, the social profitability of

Table 6.4 Real Costs in the Industrial Sector in Ghana, Ivory Coast, Senegal and Mali, 1972

Sector	Ghana Coefficient of real cost		Ivory Coast Coefficient of real cost		Senegal Coefficient of real cost		Mali Coefficient of real cost	
	Without excess profits	With excess profits	Without excess profits	With excess profits	Without excess profits	With excess profits	Without excess profits	With excess profits
Food products	1.38	4.17	-1.12	-1.18	-5.02	0.88	-7.61	-5.80
Textiles and clothing	-4.82	-1.71	-40.61	-6.45	2.43	2.10	2.30	2.40
Footwear	3.01	24.86	-2.65	5.31	—	—	6.39	6.39
Wood and paper products	-14.54	-4.26	0.17	0.24	0.89	0.90	—	—
Chemical products	1.46	1.15	12.12	-5.62	1.88	1.39	4.29	4.29
Non-metallic mineral products	-1.18	-1.01	0.61	0.62	0.43	0.36	2.93	2.93
Unfabricated metal products	0.93	1.43	-1.09	-1.76	—	—	2.19	1.83
Fabricated metal products	-0.99	-0.05	1.17	0.82	0.46	0.38	-5.28	-10.07
Vehicles	-0.62	-1.02	0.68	0.72	0.49	0.47	-8.29	-1.48
Industrial sector	1.58	3.07	1.55	2.17	0.83	1.22	5.61	5.96

Source: Balassa (1978).

manufacturing is highest in Senegal, where these industries have been established longest. In second place comes Ivory Coast, where industrial development has been rapid during the past twenty years. Ghana and Mali show overall the lowest social profitability. Indeed, in Ghana, Mali and Ivory Coast a negative coefficient is found for several sectors, implying that their activities generate a net loss of foreign exchange. In Senegal, this is the case for only one sector if excess profits are excluded. In general, the relative social profitability of industry in the four countries does not appear to be affected significantly by the inclusion or exclusion of excess profits earned by foreign enterprises, although the importance of this element varies considerably, being highest in Ghana and followed by Ivory Coast, Senegal and Mali in that order.

The detailed results for particular activities within sectors (World Bank, 1975, 1976, 1977a, b) reveal considerable differences in real costs. Balassa concludes therefore that substantial opportunities of gains from intra-Community trade could be anticipated in these cases. If trade took place according to real costs, this would be true. But intra-Community trade during the second, third and final phases of the progression towards a customs union will not be determined by domestic resource costs. Effective protection rates are a better indicator of the resource pulls that would actually result from changes in intra-Community tariffs and tariff harmonisation, because they are based on market prices rather than on shadow prices. Such rates would, of course, be subject to variation during the trade liberalisation and customs unification process even in the absence of underlying real changes in the different national economies.

Even at a national level, the use of estimates of real costs to guide development policies is subject to important limitations. These limitations are even greater in the context of a regional development strategy. They originate in both statistical and theoretical considerations.

At a purely statistical level, several limitations must be recognised: such calculations refer to a single year; they are crucially affected by the degree of capacity utilisation in that year; they rest on estimates of capital stock that may be subject to major error, as well as on other estimates, for instance of the shadow price of foreign exchange, that are notoriously difficult to make; sectors are broadly defined and, even if a finer product analysis is undertaken, an activity may still include several distinct products for some of which a country may possess an advantage, while for others it may not. Some of these problems can be allowed for in part. For instance, the World Bank estimates cited by Balassa were adjusted to allow for full capacity utilisation, thus spreading capital costs over a larger output, and for certain categories finer product breakdowns were provided. Adjustments of these kinds can reduce inherent statistical weaknesses but cannot entirely overcome them.

Domestic resource cost calculations are also subject to more fundamental limitations, which in some cases may be empirically serious. Neither ERP nor DRC calculations are applied in the context of a general equilibrium framework. For the kinds of across-the-board changes in trade taxes that are involved in trade liberalisation and tariff unification, this is in principle a serious limitation upon their practical value. If this were so in practice, and not all economists might agree (Balassa, 1982), applied general equilibrium methods of the kind discussed by Dervis, de Melo and Robinson (1982) would be more appropriate if an adequate data base were available, and if the models could be adapted for multi-country use. In the present conditions of most of West Africa's economies, it is unlikely to be necessary or feasible to take general equilibrium repercussions into account systematically.

But since the coefficients result from the operation of actual industries set up primarily to serve national markets and at different times, they have to be applied with caution. Technologies, and so costs, may differ for purely historical reasons. Scales of production are not always appropriate to the larger Community market. A DRC calculated for an industry established to serve a national market and not embodying an appropriate technology will not provide a sure guide to comparative advantage and regional specialisation.

Nevertheless, if systematic up-to-date real cost studies for at least the industrially more advanced ECOWAS countries can be produced, they may be the best attainable basis for providing broad policy guidelines, so long as appropriate allowance is made for the operation of scale economies in the context of the enlarged market (Pearson and Ingram, 1980), for the impact of transport costs, and above all, for the prospective influence of dynamic factors. The impact of the dynamic factors is particularly difficult to assess, yet it is these factors, with their implications for dynamic comparative advantage, that will ultimately be decisive.

EQUITY, COMPENSATION AND BALANCED DEVELOPMENT: THE COMMUNITY'S POLICIES

Although the Treaty gives much emphasis to measures designed to avoid the distortion of competition and to promote uniform market conditions, so giving full scope to appropriate specialisation patterns, it also gives weight to the need to promote a fair and equitable distribution of the benefits of cooperation and to eliminate disparities in the level of development of member states. Among the policies envisaged for this purpose are compensation for certain losses that may be suffered by member states in the process of trade liberalisation, and the promotion of development projects in less developed member states. The Fund for Co-operation, Compensation and Development is assigned a key role in relation to these policies or measures, although it also has more general developmental tasks. Other measures, and in particular those adopted for industrial harmonisation (including industrial incentives), may ultimately be even more crucial in determining what the Community can actually achieve in promoting a more balanced pattern of development, but in the earlier stages the Fund's contribution could be relatively important.

It is compensation that is initially in question. Compensation and other forms of assistance to member states that suffer losses as a result of the establishment of Community enterprises and revenue losses from trade liberalisation are to be provided primarily through special funds contributed by member states for this purpose. The provisions relating to compensation are to be found in Articles 25 and 50 of the Treaty, in the annexed Protocol on Compensation for Revenue Loss, and in Decision 19/5/80 of the Authority (A/DEC 19/5/80; ECOWAS, *Official Journal*, June 1980).

The Protocol on Revenue Loss provides that the loss of revenue in any year is to be assessed as equal to the difference between the total revenue that would result from the duties and taxes applicable to commodities before the coming into force of the Treaty (if they originated from a third country enjoying most favoured nation treatment), and the amount actually collected as a result of the application of the Treaty. The Protocol provides that, for its part, the exporting member state shall make compensatory payments to the Fund in respect of losses occasioned by its exports.

In 1980, the Authority agreed on a scheme to give effect to the Treaty requirements. Its provisions are as follows:

(1) The contribution of a member state to the compensation budget is calculated on the basis of the country's share in the value of total intra-Community exports of originating manufactured products.

(2) Losses of revenue resulting from preferential duties are in principle to be fully compensated for. However, for reasons of solidarity, one-fifth of the losses suffered by the four more developed countries, that is, Ivory Coast, Ghana, Nigeria and Senegal, shall be subject to redistribution. During the first five

years this amount is to be distributed to the least developed states in inverse proportion to the coefficient of the contribution of member states to the budget of the Community. After this period, this one-fifth is to be distributed to all sixteen member states in inverse proportion to their contributions to the Community budget. The conditions governing the use of the one-fifth by member states are to be determined by the Council of Ministers.

This scheme has a number of resemblances to that in force in CEAO, in particular: compensation is limited to losses in respect of manufactured products; contributions to the compensation budget are not closely linked to the nominal value of preferences received by a particular country; losses of the more developed countries are not fully compensated, but the minimum percentage of compensation as of right is higher in the case of ECOWAS (80 per cent) than in the case of CEAO (66⅔ per cent), and for the less developed members it is 100 per cent.

The rationale for compensation has already been discussed in Chapter 3 (pp. 22–4). It is not to provide compensation for tariff revenue losses *per se*. Any revenue losses imposed on a member by the process of trade liberalisation and integration that result merely from internal transfers from the state to the consumer should be recouped by a greater reliance on internal indirect taxes on goods and services. Compensation can broadly be justified to the extent that tariff revenue losses correspond to higher import outlays and therefore to the short-run or impact loss of national income that an importing country suffers when it offers a preference to a partner. Likewise, the payment of compensation by an exporting country on the basis of preferences received can be justified on the ground that the preference measures the lowest value that can attach to the benefit the exporting country receives in terms of additional national income from the opportunity to export to a partner on preferential terms.

Nevertheless, the nominal value of preferences would provide an accurate indicator of impact losses and gains only in a limiting case. In the short run, when the structure of production is fixed and capacity is given, this would be where the price of the Community product was equivalent to the cif price from the rest of the world plus the tariff. This would be so (in the absence of quantitative restrictions) only if there were a sufficiently large volume of imports from the rest of the world to set local prices. Often this is not the case because of the impact of transport costs or other geographical protection. Likewise, the external tariff may be higher than a Community product needs in order to compete. Any such 'redundant' element is irrelevant to compensation unless the Community producer is able to disregard competition in his Community market. Furthermore, quantitative restrictions also affect the pattern of trade and the margin of protection. For these and other reasons the implicit tariff that is strictly relevant to compensation must be expected to differ substantially from the nominal tariff. Detailed price comparisons would be required to determine the implicit tariff accurately, and on practical grounds these must be ruled out.

In addition to these qualifications, account must be taken of the fact that where unemployed resources exist, as is often the case within ECOWAS, producers may be able to expand their outputs as well as to improve the terms on which they sell their products to their partners. This would constitute an additional reason for concluding that the nominal value of preferences would understate the income gains to exporting countries, although the additional tax revenues generated from the expanded trade might not necessarily suffice to finance the required compensation payment.

For all these reasons, the relationship between the degree of nominal preferences accorded to a Community product and the distribution of short-run costs and benefits cannot be expected to be close. In the case of food, drink and tobacco and many traditional agricultural products, indeed, it may be that no excess cost is incurred, the product of ECOWAS partners being, in some cases, cheaper than imports from third countries. Nevertheless to the extent that import revenue losses correspond to the impact losses imposed upon member states by the preferences they offer and receive, and full compensation is paid for such losses, member states would be no better off than without trade liberalisation. In the longer run, member states could expect to benefit from any integration-induced development and growth in the Community, and it is, of course, a principal *raison d'être* of the Community to bring about such development.

In a purely competitive situation, however, the less developed and the less industrialised member states would not be well placed to profit from such opportunities. Their benefits, if any, must therefore be expected to be derived principally from one or more of three sources: 'overcompensation' (that is, receipts in excess of effective revenue losses); differential assistance provided through the Fund in other ways (that is, for the promotion of industrial projects in LDC member states); and other Community policies designed to promote balanced development, including the harmonisation of fiscal and industrial policies. In this sense, the extent of the contribution to equitable development that can be made by the ECOWAS Fund from its own financial resources depends largely, at the present time, on the current provisions for compensation and on the pace and character of trade liberalisation, which jointly determine the available special funds. Even if trade liberalisation proceeds as rapidly as has been agreed, the initial scope for rendering the operations of the Community attractive to the less developed or less industrialised members by means of redistributive transfers (that is, by overcompensation) must necessarily be very limited as long as a high level of compensation is automatically provided for revenue losses irrespective of 'need'.

The use of the 'special' resources of the Fund for trade-related redistributive purposes (that is, for 'overcompensation') raises political and practical difficulties. First, commonly used entitlement indicators such as GNP *per capita* and population estimates are often inaccurate. The large adjustments made recently by the World Bank in the GNP *per capita* estimates for Ghana and Mauretania and in the population estimates for Guinea (World Bank, 1982b) well illustrate the problems. Secondly, even within a relatively homogeneous region such as the Community, GNP *per capita* at official exchange rates is an unsatisfactory indicator of relative levels of development. Thirdly, intra-Community trade statistics are at present only available after a considerable lapse of time. Even within the six-country Community of the Abidjan Treaty, the statistical problems are immense, and delays and adjustments make it impossible to close the Fund's accounts within a reasonable period of time. A strong statistical service will almost certainly be needed in ECOWAS at Community level to underpin its compensation scheme, and both at Community and at national levels computerisation might be a virtual precondition for its successful operation. Finally, the Community has no 'own resources' to operate the scheme and will be dependent on the prompt payment by member states of their assessed contributions. The experience of CEAO – and indeed of ECOWAS itself in other areas – makes it obvious that promptness in meeting financial obligations towards the Community cannot yet be invariably relied upon.

It is ironic that ECOWAS should have adopted a compensation scheme that, however logical and equitable it may be, depends on the paying-over of resources by the member countries out of their budgets, just at a time when CEAO for its part has been led – because of the self-same difficulties – to think of moving to an alternative system of financial compensation. Of course, there is ultimately no way of avoiding the burden by any conceivable fiscal alternative, but the provision of own resources for both CEAO and ECOWAS in respect of compensation arrangements would have several important advantages. The practical problems will be given no further mention here.

THE DISTRIBUTIONAL IMPLICATIONS OF TRADE LIBERALISATION AND COMPENSATION

The eventual distributional implications of any compensation scheme in ECOWAS will depend, in the medium term, on the impact of trade liberalisation. A realistic estimate of the trade and distributional impact of liberalisation cannot at present be made because of ignorance as to the relevant elasticities, the dominating influence in many instances of non-tariff barriers, the difficulty of determining which products would actually qualify for liberalisation in terms of the Community's complex rules of origin, the lack of relevant estimates of effective protection rates, and the lack of correspondence between the value of preferences received and contributions to the compensation budget.

The only practicable means of illustrating the prospective financial implications of compensation in ECOWAS and the issues presented is to follow a taxonomic approach. For this purpose, attention will be focused on intra-ECOWAS trade with the exclusion of intra-CEAO trade, since special arrangements operate within the latter. Only trade in manufactures will be considered since, as in CEAO, compensation in ECOWAS is limited to losses arising from this component of trade.

Table 6.5 shows recorded intra-ECOWAS trade and trade balances in manufactures (that is, excluding mineral and agricultural products) for non-CEAO trade for the latest available year. On the basis of this table, the effect of varying degrees of trade liberalisation and trade expansion accompanied by alternative redistributive schemes can be illustrated. It will be assumed: (1) that the relevant tariff on imports is 50 per cent, excluding non-discriminatory fiscal duties; (2) that all recorded trade in manufactures would qualify for Community treatment, although it seems likely that, if present origin rules are applied, practically none would so qualify; (3) that the compensation budget is equal to 100 per cent of revenue losses.

It is first assumed that revenue losses are to be fully compensated. With complete trade liberalisation, but no trade expansion, gross assessed contributions to the Fund would, on the basis of the 1975 figures, amount to about $20m. If 100 per cent compensation for revenue losses is paid to all states, the major net exporters would contribute net some $10m. of which Ivory Coast would provide nearly three-quarters, and Senegal most of the balance. The principal net beneficiaries would be Nigeria and Ghana, which together would receive about three-quarters of the net redistributed sum, while The Gambia and Mauretania would receive much of the balance. For purposes of comparison it may be noted that gross contributions to

Table 6.5 *Intra-ECOWAS Trade in Manufactures (Excluding Intra-CEAO Trade), 1975 ($m.)*

Country	Trade in manufactured goods		
	Exports	Imports	Balance
Ivory Coast	15.6	0.9	+14.7
Senegal	(5.0)	(0.8)	(+4.2)
Liberia	3.7	0.9	+2.8
Sierra Leone	(1.0)	(0.5)	(+0.5)
Benin	(6.0)	(6.2)	(−0.2)
Upper Volta	0.1	0.9	−0.8
Togo	4.5	4.6	−0.1
Niger	1.1	1.2	−0.1
Mali	0.1	0.4	−0.3
Mauretania	—	2.2	−2.2
The Gambia	—	1.9	−1.9
Ghana	3.2	6.6	−3.4
Guinea	—	(0.3)	(−0.3)
Nigeria	0.3	11.5	−11.2

Notes: Figures in brackets represent estimates. Data for Guinea–Bissau and Cape Verde not available.
Source: Trade statistics based on UNCTAD data.

CEAO's compensation fund were assessed for 1976 at 2m. fr. CFA, which is approximately equivalent to $10m.

If it is assumed that intra-Community trade would expand by 200 per cent over the relevant period, the payments and receipts just referred to would have to be increased by that factor. Gross contributions would then amount to some $60m. but, assuming equiproportionate expansion of the exports and imports of each member state, the inter-country distribution of the expanded net payments would not be affected.

These indicative calculations depend crucially on the specific assumptions that have been made about margins of preference, tariff levels and the country distribution of trade expansion. Alternative assumptions about rates of preference and import duty levels would yield different magnitudes, but nothing will alter the fact that, if 100 per cent compensation for revenue losses is paid as of right, the scope for discretionary redistributive payments through the Fund would be nil. Only if compensation were to be paid at less than 100 per cent could funds be set free to form a distributive pool that could be used to produce net benefits for the less advanced members of the Community.

As has already been pointed out (pp. 106–7) the compensation scheme adopted by the Community in 1980 does embody a redistributive element. Compensation for revenue losses for its more developed member states – namely, Ivory Coast, Ghana, Nigeria and Senegal – is to be limited to 80 per cent. The resulting balance is then to be distributed for the initial five years, to the least developed states in proportions inversely related to their share of the Community's budget. Subsequently, the balance is to be distributed to all member states in inverse proportion to their contributions to the Community budget.

The financial impact of this scheme can be gauged, again using the trade matrix for 1975. On the assumptions being made, the gross contributions to the Fund would not be affected. The difference would lie solely in the basis on which distributions from the Fund are assumed to be made. Table 6.6 shows the net contributions and recalculated receipts, again assuming no trade expansion and a situation of complete trade liberalisation. These indicative calculations illustrate the purely formal redistributive effects of alternative compensation arrangements in terms of the recorded trade flows in ECOWAS in 1975. Whether a scheme on such lines is judged to be equitable must be considered with reference not to its formal financial incidence, but to its effective incidence, for it is the latter that will largely determine the resulting distribution of the burdens and benefits.

It will be clear from the analysis on pages 107–9 that the effective incidence of such compensation arrangements largely depends upon the resulting price changes of benefiting products. If it is assumed that export prices rise to the full extent of the accorded tariff preference then, although exporting countries might lose public revenues from their obligation to pay compensation, they would not lose real domestic product, as compared with their pre-liberalisation positions. If substantial trade expansion should occur with liberalisation, they might not even suffer a loss of public revenues. On the other hand, irrespective of the degree of trade expansion, importing countries would always require full compensation for revenue losses if they were not to be made worse off by preferential trade.

Balassa has claimed (1978, p. 11) that available information does in fact suggest that prices established in intra-regional trade are largely determined by the price of imports from third countries plus the tariff. If so, any redistribution of resources to the less advanced members of ECOWAS financed by departing from 100 per cent compensation would imply that the real burden of compensation would be largely borne by the better-off net importing countries, with Nigeria making the largest contribution. Although Ivory Coast and Senegal would benefit in terms of increased domestic product from

Table 6.6 Compensation for ECOWAS Trade Liberalisation in Manufactures ($m.)

Country	Assessed contribution[a]	Revenue loss compensation[b]	Distributive pool for all except*[c]	Total distribution	Net contribution (−) or receipt (+)
CEAO:					
Ivory Coast*	7.80	0.36	—	0.36	−7.44
Upper Volta	0.05	0.45	0.20	0.65	+0.60
Mali	0.05	0.20	0.20	0.40	+0.35
Mauretania	—	1.10	0.20	1.30	+1.30
Niger	0.50	0.60	0.40	1.00	+0.50
Senegal*	2.50	0.32	—	0.32	−2.18
Mano River Union					
Guinea	—	0.10	0.20	0.30	+0.30
Liberia	1.80	0.45	0.20	0.65	−1.15
Sierra Leone	0.50	0.25	0.20	0.45	−0.05
Other ECOWAS countries[d]					
Benin	3.00	3.10	0.20	3.30	+0.30
Ghana*	1.60	2.60	—	2.60	+1.00
Nigeria*	0.20	4.60	—	4.60	+4.40
Togo	2.20	2.30	0.20	2.50	+0.30
The Gambia	—	0.90	0.02	0.92	(+0.92)
Total[e]	20.20	18.20	2.00	(20.20)	—

Notes: [a]Total value of the assumed 50% tariff allocated according to shares of exports of manufactures.
[b]80% of assessed revenue losses in the case of the more advanced countries (starred), and 100% in all other cases.
[c]Distributable to less developed members only in inverse proportion to contribution to ECOWAS budget. For simplicity, here distributed according to relative GDP.
[d]Data for Guinea–Bissau and Cape Verde not available.
[e]Totals may not add to the sum of individual items due to rounding and discrepancies in trade statistics.

more favourable prices for their exports and, further, from any trade expansion, they would not in such circumstances effectively bear any real burden.

If, alternatively, it were assumed that the prices of benefiting exports do not rise by the full amount of the preference, either in the short or the long run, then with full compensation Ivory Coast and Senegal would each effectively bear some of the real as well as the nominal financial burden of compensation. By the same token, the payment of 'full' compensation to any importing country would imply a real redistribution in their favour – that is, effectively, 'overcompensation'.

The adoption by ECOWAS of a compensation scheme similar to that of CEAO should minimise the problem of assimilating the two arrangements, and enable ECOWAS to profit from CEAO's considerable operating experience. But the context of intra-group trade in ECOWAS is at present quite different from that in CEAO. In the first place, individual CEAO countries largely determine for themselves (through the TCR) the extent to which they are prepared to experience trade creation or trade diversion as a result of integration. This will not be the case in ECOWAS if its presently envisaged trade liberalisation arrangements are implemented. Secondly, whereas in CEAO the principal net importers are the poorer states, in ECOWAS, by contrast, the principal net importer of manufactures is one of the wealthiest states – Nigeria. Until this changes, the provision of compensation on the agreed basis would principally result in the establishment of a complex system of transfers that would largely operate among the wealthier states. The scope for benefiting the Community's less developed members would be small. Of course, if trade expansion takes place amongst the wealthier states, this would increase the scope for assisting theLDCs through these special funds, but substantial expansion would have to occur before any significant contribution would be made, given the presently envisaged levels of 'automatic' compensation. Even by comparison with CEAO's fund, which is not itself particularly generous, the ECOWAS scheme would not rate very highly. In most cases it seems that the less developed members of ECOWAS would hardly attain the level of overcompensation (in *per capita* terms) to which comparable imports would entitle them if the CEAO base were in force.

IMPLEMENTING THE TREATY

The Community's activities began slowly, and its first four years were largely devoted to institution-building and to putting flesh on the bones of the Treaty. All progress was at first blocked for eighteen months by attempts on the part of Ivory Coast and Senegal to make the adoption of the first five crucial protocols conditional upon the broadening of ECOWAS to include the francophone states of Central Africa, including Zaire. This attempt, clearly motivated by fear of Nigerian hegemony (Ojo, 1980), was successfully opposed by Nigeria and, at the second summit meeting in November 1976, all five protocols were signed. (Protocols 1–5 deal respectively with: the rules of origin; the transfer within ECOWAS of goods imported from third countries; the assessment of loss of revenue; the Fund for Co-operation, Compensation and Development; contributions to the ECOWAS budget.) Since 1979, more progress has been discernible. Much necessary groundwork has been undertaken and a number of important protocols and decisions have been adopted.

The substantive implementation of the Treaty may be said to have commenced in May 1979 with the belated coming into force of the standstill provision of the Treaty, following the fourth summit meeting. This provision obliges member states to refrain for a two-year period from imposing new customs duties or taxes and from increasing existing ones. It marks the first of the three stages of the envisaged trade liberalisation process. The second stage, involving the reduction of tariff and non-tariff barriers and scheduled to be completed in eight years, should have begun two years later, in May 1981.

In order to bring the second stage into operation, several preliminary steps were required: (1) the determination of a schedule for trade liberalisation; (2) the adoption of a compensation scheme for revenue loss that is associated with the trade liberalisation programme and operates in parallel with it; and (3) the adoption of certain limited measures of fiscal harmonisation.

The initial decision on trade liberalisation (A/DEC 18/5/80; ECOWAS, *Official Journal,* No. 2, 1980) divides both products and countries into two groups. The member states designated as industrially more advanced – namely, Ivory Coast, Ghana, Nigeria and Senegal – are required to eliminate their tariff barriers over the period 1981–6. Other member states are not required to eliminate their tariffs until 1988. Priority industrial products are to be liberalised according to an accelerated schedule (four years for the industrially more advanced, six years for the others). Other products are to be liberalised over a six-year period in the case of the industrially more advanced members and eight years in the case of the others.

It is the list of priority industrial products (contained in the annex to Council Decision C/DEC 3/5/82) that is of immediate interest. The list includes most manufactured food products, certain building materials, mineral fuels, pharmaceutical products, fertilisers, plastic materials, rubber articles, wood articles, ceramic products, iron and steel products and certain agricultural machinery. Many major products are not included in the list, notably those of the widely important textile and clothing industries.

The initial decision on trade liberalisation also required all member states to eliminate their non-tariff barriers within a four-year period from 28 May 1981. However, the subsequent amplificatory Council decision of May 1982 (C/DEC 4/5/82) contains the significant reservation that foreign exchange restrictions on current transactions shall only be eliminated after the problems of currency convertibility have been resolved.

The scheme for compensation for revenue loss was agreed at the May 1980 meetings (A/DEC 17/5/80 and A/DEC 19/5/80). It provides for the payment through the ECOWAS Fund of compensation for revenue losses arising out of the process of trade liberalisation (strictly tariff liberalisation). Compensation is to be paid out of funds contributed by member states in proportion to their shares of intra-Community exports of manufactures. The industrially less advanced members are to receive full compensation for their revenue losses plus, for an initial five-year period, an additional sum. The additional 'redistributive' element is to be financed initially by restricting the compensation paid to the industrially more advanced members to 80 per cent of their assessed revenue losses.

In the course of the eight-year period of trade liberalisation that constitutes the second phase of the Community's move towards a customs union, member states are also required, under Article 17 of the Treaty, to modify their internal indirect taxes so that the products of other Community members are not subjected to higher rates than those imposed upon comparable domestic products. This provision is necessary to avoid the competitive distortions that could otherwise be produced by the imposition of indirect taxes that, although formally internal, would effectively in part have the character of an import duty.

The implementation of this provision, and indeed of the trade liberalisation programme itself, confronts serious difficulties because of the lack of a uniform Community system of customs and of internal indirect taxes, and from the lack of a clear distinction in the tax systems of several member states between import duties and internal indirect taxes. Effectively, the anglophone member states and some francophone member states do not distinguish in their customs tariffs between import duties proper and customs duty elements that, being the counterpart to equivalent domestic fiscal charges on local products, are to be considered as internal indirect taxes. The situation is further complicated because in a number of francophone countries there exist several different kinds of import duty, some of which, though the counterparts of internal duties, are not necessarily levied on an identical base or at identical rates. The lack of a harmonised fiscal structure has already produced difficulties in the standstill period. Similar, but more acute difficulties are likely to arise in the course of the ensuing trade liberalisation phase.

A few member states of the Community have already dealt with the problem of discrimination in their internal indirect tax systems in the context of their membership of CEAO, where discrimination is similarly ruled out. Likewise, in CEAO a measure of fiscal harmonisation in terms of tax structures and nomenclatures, essentially motivated by the requirements of trade liberalisation and the prospective move towards a common external tariff, has been agreed. Although the extent and degree of discrimination from this source is probably not a major problem in ECOWAS at present, it does occur, for instance in the systems of Benin, Guinea and Togo, and for certain other countries it is found in respect of particular products.

It is evidently desirable that ECOWAS should adopt as soon as possible a common structure and nomenclature for all indirect taxes in the Community that would at least make a clear distinction between import duties and internal indirect taxes. This would facilitate the implementation of the trade liberalisation programme and the identification of possible instances of discrimination. It would also facilitate the changes that will be required in the third phase of the liberalisation programme when the Community is to progress towards a common external tariff. The measures of fiscal harmonisation in CEAO exemplify what needs to be done. Action in ECOWAS on somewhat similar lines has been under consideration since 1980, but no decisions have yet been reached except for a comparatively minor one of May 1982 – that permits member states to replace elements of their customs tariffs that are in effect internal indirect taxes by an appropriate sales tax.

During the second stage of the trade liberalisation programme, the member states will retain their own national tariffs. At its conclusion, when all tariffs have been eliminated on intra-Community trade, ECOWAS will be a *de facto* free trade area. In any integration scheme, but in particular one in which, initially, national tariffs are high and disparate, rules of origin are extremely important. It is no accident that the First Protocol to the Treaty is concerned with the rules that determine a product's eligibility for treatment as a Community product.

The matter has since occupied the institutions of the Community on several occasions. Apart from fairly orthodox requirements in terms of value-added within the Community (since 1979 a minimum of 35 per cent of ex-factory value is required for eligibility), the First Protocol also contains a more unusual prescription requiring a minimum level of participation by nationals of ECOWAS countries in the equity of industrial enterprises as a further necessary condition for eligibility for Community treatment. At the May 1980 summit, the required minimum levels of participation were specified to be 20 per cent by 28 May 1981; 35 per cent by May 1983; and 51 per cent by May 1989. At these ownership levels, most Nigerian products would be eligible for treatment as Community products in terms of the requirements of its indigenisation legislation. To a considerable but lesser extent, the same would appear to be true of Ghana. But for Ivory Coast and Senegal, where local equity participation in local branches of multinational enterprises is still, as a matter of policy, on a limited scale, these requirements could currently be met only for a limited number of the largest industrial establishments. Since Ivory Coast and Senegal at present account for a high proportion of the manufactured exports amongst Community members, this ownership provision will ensure that the trade liberalisation provisions of ECOWAS will remain largely without practical effect until such time as the affected member states are able and willing to comply with the ownership provisions, or these provisions are modified.

All of the measures described above are concerned with the customs and trade matters that form the subject of Chapter 3 of the Treaty of Lagos. When it comes to other aspects of the Treaty, and in particular to the foreshadowed measures of positive economic integration and policy harmonisation, there is less progress to report.

Initiatives have been taken in a number of areas. As a first step towards the projected abolition of obstacles to the free movement of persons, services and capital, steps have been taken to abolish visas and entry permits for short stays. A special fund for telecommunications has been established that is annexed to the ECOWAS Fund. Its purpose is to guarantee loans and make subventions for the improvement of telecommunications. A voluntary fund has similarly been established for energy resources development. A defence pact has been mooted but has so far failed to materialise. In a separate initiative, a West African Clearing House was decided upon in 1974. Following its expansion to cover all ECOWAS members with the exception of Cape Verde, this body, together with its *alter ego* the Committee of West African Central Banks, performs for ECOWAS several of the functions in respect of monetary cooperation that are envisaged in Articles 37 and 39 of the Treaty. Under its aegis and in consultation with the ECOWAS Secretariat, the problems of currency convertibility, which are crucial to trade liberalisation, have been subjected to increasing attention.

No significant progress has yet been made on the measures and policies for positive integration – in particular, industrial and fiscal harmonisation – that formed such an important ingredient of the Treaty of Lagos. Inaction in such important policy areas has been a frequent source of difficulty in other Third World groupings. Signs are not lacking that the postponement of most action in these areas to later stages of the Community's operations, as envisaged in the Treaty, may present serious obstacles to the progress of the Community's trade liberalisation programme.

PROBLEMS AND PROSPECTS

Since its establishment, the Community has built up much of the necessary institutional framework required for establishing a customs union. A range of important protocols needed to give effect to treaty provisions in respect of trade and customs have been adopted, thus giving operational content to some of the more general provisions of the Treaty. In the Fund for Co-operation, Compensation and Development, the Community possesses an institution of potentially great importance for promoting positive integration, development and balance. In purely institutional terms the way has thus been opened for concrete beneficial advances. There are nevertheless crucial weaknesses in the present procedures of the Community that will have to be resolved soon if benefits are to be realised and further progress is not to be held up. Essentially these weaknesses stem from two aspects: (1) the lack of an agreed development strategy for the Community; and (2) the lack of simultaneity in the obligations and benefits imposed by the Community's programmes.

The Community clearly lacks a concrete development and industrialisation strategy. In a general sense, no doubt, the Community might be said to have a strategy, since its emphasis on the promotion of uniform market conditions is tantamount to giving primacy to competitive forces. But the framework within which competition will operate is as yet completely undetermined because of the absence of an agreed general structure of protection (to be provided through the common external tariff and investment incentives). In the transitional stage before external tariffs are harmonised, the resource allocation and developmental effects of the Community will be largely determined by the fortuitous impact of trade liberalisation that is being undertaken against the background of national protective structures that are generally very high but also diverse and that have not been constructed with the requirements of a regional market in mind. There are no *a priori* grounds for supposing that the trade that is induced against this background will necessarily be favourable in terms of its resource allocation and developmental implications. Indeed, those effects could well be adverse.

In this respect the Community's situation differs considerably from that in certain other free trade areas, such as EFTA, where tariffs were generally much lower and disparities in effective protection much less extreme, or in Central America, where trade liberalisation was conditional on prior tariff harmonisation.

Although the distributive effects resulting from trade liberalisation in this rather unsatisfactory context should be partly offset by the Community's compensation scheme, that in itself cannot justify the pattern of trade and resource allocation that will result, which still remains essentially unappraised; and it does nothing to mitigate the distortions in resource allocation that may be encouraged not only in the exporting countries but also in the importing countries during the process.

The justification for embarking on complete trade liberalisation prior to the adoption of a common external tariff is in itself obscure, if not dubious. It must presumably rest on the proposition either that the resulting distortions will not be significant, or that functionalist considerations would nevertheless justify incurring them in the interest of accelerating the integration process. It is difficult to make such a judgement since data relevant to the implied trade-off are not available. If severe resource misallocations should be produced in the trade liberalisation phase of the move to a customs union, obstacles to further integration may well be strengthened rather than overcome. At the present time, however, the point is academic, since the formal implementation of the Community's trade liberalisation programme is unlikely to have much practical effect – except to necessitate interbudgetary transfer payments – because the impact of the Community's rules of origin would currently prevent significant trade expansion, even if foreign exchange restrictions did not.

The integration strategy that the Community has adopted – namely, to agree on a very broad framework within which detailed integration policies can subsequently be worked out – was, no doubt, appropriate and indeed inevitable, but it does demand a careful ordering of procedures and stages if it is to be constructive. In certain respects, alternative procedures to those now being followed would be far less prone to generate difficulties.

This is particularly so with respect to the lack of simultaneity in obligations and benefits that was mentioned above. This is an aspect that affects the less industrially advanced member countries above all, although to some extent it is relevant to all. Despite the emphasis on protecting the interests of the less advanced member states, the

Treaty cannot be regarded as adequately doing so. The timetabled obligations on the customs union constitute measures from which, on balance, the industrially less advanced members are unlikely to benefit. Of those measures from which they might expect to benefit – namely, redistributive compensation; differential action through the Fund to promote their industrialisation; and fiscal and industrial harmonisation – only the first is timetabled, and it is insignificant. The others remain to be made concrete.

It is true that the Community's trade liberalisation programme provides for the payment of compensation for revenue losses. This should remove some of the transitional costs for the less advanced members and for others. But the scheme does not compensate for the contingent losses from trade creation, which – in the absence of an effective Community regional policy – could be significant, or for the important constraints on development policy that the acceptance of the programme will necessarily impose upon them. In these circumstances, the less advanced countries may justifiably be tempted to hang back from implementing formal commitments to trade liberalisation until they are assured, either through the ECOWAS Fund or in other ways, that their interests will be fully safeguarded.

It is important to recognise that in this respect the situation of ECOWAS is quite different from that in CEAO, which is possibly more logical. An effective regional industrialisation programme is also lacking in CEAO but, pending its introduction, member states are not obliged to accept full trade liberalisation. Each member can avoid trade creation, and potential damage to its own industries, by fixing appropriate TCR rates. Against that background, the CEAO compensation scheme is not unsatisfactory. In the context of ECOWAS however, given full trade liberalisation, the Community's scheme would only be equitable if other positive integration measures operating in favour of the less advanced members are brought into operation. In short, in the context of automatic full trade liberalisation operating in isolation from other measures, ECOWAS needs a more generous compensation scheme than that of CEAO; it has adopted a less generous one.

In principle, pending differential action through the Fund and other positive measures, it would be possible to deal with the fears of the less advanced members of ECOWAS in several ways: they could, by the authorisation of a device such as the TCR, be permitted to postpone full liberalisation until such time as, by industrial and fiscal harmonisation or direct action through the Fund's ordinary resources, the positive measures of ECOWAS come into operation in their favour – in this way, the interests of less advanced member states could be fully protected; they could be permitted to operate less restrictive rules of origin; they might be permitted to enter into transitional bilateral trade agreements involving balanced trade expansion, although these are at present specifically excluded by the trade liberalisation decisions of 1982.

The strategic question for policy-makers, of course, is whether approaches on such lines would encourage the integration process or would merely result in a low and static level of economic cooperation. It is no doubt a tenable viewpoint that, if trade liberalisation is introduced without concomitant regional policies, irresistible pressures would be produced to implement such measures promptly because the alternative would not be stability at the low level of cooperation then attained but almost certainly a politically damaging collapse. But experience in other groupings suggests that this may be a high-risk policy.

Other potential problems for ECOWAS are not unrelated to the issues here discussed, notably that of the smaller groupings within ECOWAS such as MRU and CEAO and the Senegambian Confederation. The implementation of Article 20 of the Treaty requiring the extension of most favoured nation treatment to other member states is a case in point. The smaller groups cannot be expected to favour a weakening of their own special arrangements – some of which incorporate built-in safeguards – until ECOWAS shows concrete signs of developing effectual measures for industrial and fiscal harmonisation.

The impact of such difficulties and of other unresolved and sometimes unexpressed differences in the developmental objectives of member states appears largely to account for the current situation in which, as President Shagari of Nigeria has remarked, 'protocols and decisions are not being ratified as fast as reasonably expected. Even those ratified are hardly implemented to the spirit and letter' (*Africa Research Bulletin,* 1980, Vol. 19, No. 5, p. 6440). ECOWAS now has a comprehensive set of programmes in the field of trade and customs, with the significant exception of the common external tariff. Its trade liberalisation programme appears to be on the verge of becoming operational. At this stage, the Community appears to have a choice between a high-risk strategy of securing formal commitments to the existing liberalisation programme in the hope that concomitant measures required to provide the Community with a coherent set of policies can subsequently be implemented before present inconsistencies and inadequacies become too manifest, or alternatively accepting that the programme needs to be modified. Desirable ingredients of an alternative strategy would be built-in incentives to attain balanced development, or else safeguards that the less developed members can independently operate in the prior phase of negative integration, perhaps on the lines of those found in CEAO. Given proper leadership, such a programme might provide a better framework within which functionalist integrative forces could operate. The strategy of promoting trade liberalisation along the present lines without concomitantly phased positive policies promises to be a recipe for stagnation. In any event, a reconsideration of strategy and procedures seems urgently necessary if the integration process of the Community is to be given a renewed momentum and an improved course. An expanded role for the ECOWAS Fund should be an important ingredient of a new deal.

7 Senegambia: Economic and Monetary Union

Of the four current initiatives for economic integration in West Africa, the most recent stems from the political decision of the presidents of Senegal and The Gambia in December 1981 to establish a Senegambian confederation that is to be based *inter alia* on the establishment of an economic and monetary union between the two countries. This chapter reviews the background to this initiative and the economic issues involved, some of which are rather special.

THE HISTORICAL BACKGROUND TO CONFEDERATION

The Republic of The Gambia owes its existence entirely to colonial policy, but even by the standards of the rest of Africa its boundaries are extraordinary. It forms an irrational intrusion into the very much larger country of Senegal, stretching from the coast inland along both sides of the Gambia River to form a strip some 322 km long and only 19–21 km wide. Its frontiers roughly follow the course of the river, but they do not reach the natural limits of the river basin on either side, nor do they extend to the source of the river itself, which lies in Guinea. The frontiers of The Gambia not only cut through natural features, they also cut across human settlement patterns. Wholly surrounded by Senegal, except on its seaward margin, The Gambia largely isolates the southern region of Casamance from the rest of Senegal. Ethnically the peoples of the two countries are of similar stock. For a brief period, from 1765 to 1783, much of what are now The Gambia and Senegal formed the single British colony of Senegambia. From that time until their independence in the 1960s, the two countries have been subjected to the separate influences of the French and British colonial systems. This has created administrative, cultural, economic and monetary differences that have been and continue to be important obstacles to the closer association of the two countries.

The anomalous position of The Gambia received much attention in the nineteenth century and there were several abortive British and

French proposals to exchange some other French colony for The Gambia, so as to permit its incorporation into Senegal. Economic factors influenced these proposals, although on both sides wider issues of areas of colonial influence and general colonial policy played the major role.

Following Senegal's independence in 1960 and the prospect of early independence for The Gambia, there was a renewed interest in the possibility of closer relationships. This stemmed from three main considerations. The first was doubt as to whether The Gambia alone could be economically viable. At that time the country had a budget deficit and was dependent upon a substantial grant-in-aid from the UK. The second was the view that the economic frontier is disadvantageous for both countries. For Senegal, it means a partial isolation of its southern province of Casamance, an inability to exploit the Gambia River fully, an inability to sell its manufactures to The Gambia, and revenue losses from smuggled goods arising from The Gambia's low tariffs and the impossibility of effectively policing the borders. For The Gambia, the principal disadvantage is that it cannot exploit the river basin that is its main natural asset; Banjul (formerly Bathurst) is thus deprived of the opportunity to provide port and ancillary services for a large economic region including neighbouring parts of Senegal and nearby inland states that it is otherwise particularly well placed to serve. In short, it was argued that it would not be possible to utilise and develop the economic resources of The Gambia and Senegal optimally without close economic cooperation. A third reason for seeking association was political. There was concern in Senegal that Gambia might become a base for the operations of banned political parties or for subversion from outside. For its part, The Gambia, which lacked an army, recognised its military vulnerability.

The possibilities of association began to be explored towards the end of 1961, when the two countries established an inter-ministerial committee to discuss matters of joint interest. Among other things this committee considered such matters as cooperation and posts, telecommunications and feeder roads. Subsequently the two governments discussed the possibility that when The Gambia achieved independence a formal association between the two countries might be established. In these initial discussions the Gambian government made it clear that it would only consider association on terms that would guarantee it a high degree of autonomy in internal affairs – which amounted in effect to a willingness to consider only a weak confederal relationship. These discussions resulted in the commisioning through the UN of a report to consider the implications of alternative forms of political and economic association.

Following the submission of the UN report in March 1964 (Gambia, 1964), talks between the two governments were held in Dakar in May. At these meetings the Gambians put forward their proposals for political cooperation. These envisaged a confederal structure vested with responsibility for defence, foreign affairs and overseas representation. This limited proposal did not go far enough for Senegal, which countered with proposals envisaging the eventual integration of The Gambia into Senegal. This in its turn was not acceptable to The Gambia.

As to economic cooperation, the Gambian view at that time was that its levels of taxation and import duties should be gradually aligned with those of Senegal, thus meeting the latter's complaints about smuggling, but only if there were an assurance of countervailing benefits that would result in increased trade and economic activity in The Gambia. The Senegalese view was that any acceptable form of economic association must lead in the not too distant future to the full political incorporation of The Gambia into Senegal.

The principal outcome of the 1964 meetings was the adoption of potentially important agreements on foreign policy, covering diplomatic representation and the harmonisation of policy, and on defence, which provided for mutual assistance in the event of external aggression. The joint ministerial committee was continued. Between 1964 and 1981 not much occurred to alter the framework of agreement and consultation laid down in the 1964 meetings, although the opportunity was taken on several occasions to confirm the substance of earlier agreements. A formal treaty of association was signed in Banjul in 1967 that was intended to promote and extend coordination and cooperation between The Gambia and Senegal in all fields. In accordance with its provisions, a Senegalo-Gambian Permanent Secretariat was set up in Banjul one year later. Its purpose was to make a reality of the broad agreements arrived at by the political leadership. Within the framework of these arrangements several minor agreements have been adopted on matters such as health, broadcasting, cultural affairs and marine rescue operations (Senegalo-Gambian Permanent Secretariat, 1976). Also, in 1970 a trade agreement was concluded and subsequently in 1973 a preference margin – most often $2\frac{1}{2}$ per cent – was established by The Gambia for a wide range of Senegalese manufactured products. In 1976 a convention was signed for the establishment of a coordinating committee for the development of the Gambia river basin. This became, in 1978, the Gambia River Development Organisation (OMVG), of which Guinea is also a member. On the whole, the results of cooperation between The Gambia and Senegal during the past two decades have been modest and no greater than those achieved by many countries lacking formal treaties or permanent machinery of cooperation.

To a considerable extent, the lack of progress during this period reflects a new phase in Gambian foreign policy, which was ushered in by the 'border crisis' of 1969–71 (Hughes, 1974). It has been characterised by a certain reserve on the part of The Gambia towards Senegambian association and an interest in developing broader regional links. Although the continued importance of the Senegal connection has, not surprisingly, been expressly emphasised by President Jawara, relations with Senegal at the economic level have increasingly been seen in the context of the participation of both countries in a wider economic grouping. Unlike Senegal, Gambia had openly supported the Nigeria–Togo initiative of 1973, which aimed at the formation of an all-West African economic grouping and which subsequently led to the foundation of ECOWAS to which both countries now belong.

In an earlier study of the problems of integration between Senegal and The Gambia, it was concluded that:

In a situation in which Senegal seems committed to ultimate political integration as a condition of economic association and Gambia to substantial political autonomy, and in which the economic gains from integration are likely to be modest, the *status quo* could well continue indefinitely in the absence of fresh politically-motivated initiatives. (Robson, 1968)

In 1981, the political factor decisively supervened. Following an attempted coup d'état in The Gambia in July, President Jawara invoked the defence agreement with Senegal. Senegalese forces entered The Gambia and rapidly suppressed the coup. Shortly afterwards, the two presidents took a political decision to establish a confederation including an economic and monetary union, and their proposals were ratified by their respective parliaments soon afterwards (Gambia, 1981b).

The Confederation Agreement of 1981 provides that, while each state is to maintain its independence and sovereignty, the Confederation is to be based on: the integration of the armed forces and the security forces; coordination of external policy; coordination of policy in telecommunications and other fields to be agreed; and the development of an economic and monetary union. No timescale is established for the implementation of the Agreement. However, in July 1982, three protocols were signed covering the institutions of the Confederation, the coordination of policy in the field of external relations, and the financial regulations of the Confederation. The Senegal government, which has taken most of the early initiatives, has also submitted draft protocols on the establishment of a customs union and a monetary union, which were still under consideration at the end of 1982.

In important respects, the economic context has changed considerably for the two countries since integration was first considered. Both countries have suffered severely from the world international crisis during the past decade. In the past three years, they have both resorted to stand-by assistance from the International Monetary Fund and are implementing adjustment programmes. Both countries became members of ECOWAS in 1975, and in the framework of that Community they are committed to an eventual alignment of their economic policies in important respects. Senegal had previously become a member of CEAO, and has been a member of the West African Monetary Union since its establishment in 1962, reaffirming its commitment to the Union in 1973. What, in the present context, are the economic and monetary issues of integration between the two countries and the respective economic interests of the partner states?

THE ECONOMIC SETTING FOR ECONOMIC AND MONETARY UNION

Salient aspects of the economic structure, trade and development patterns of the two countries that are relevant to their integration are summarily discussed in the following section. Comparative data on the two economies are set out in Table 7.1.

Table 7.1 *Senegambia: The Economic Background, 1980*

Economic features	The Gambia	Senegal
Area ('000 sq.km)	11	196
Population (m.)	0.6	5.7
Rate of population increase, 1970–80 (%)	3.0[a]	2.8
Density of population per sq.km	54.5	29.1
Gross national product ($m.)	150	2,560
GNP *per capita* ($)	250	450
GNP *per capita*, real average annual growth, 1960–80 (%)	1.7	−0.3
Groundnut produce as percentage of recorded merchandise exports	85	63

[a]1970–9.
Sources: World Bank (1982a,b); Gambia (1981a).

In size, the two countries are very different. In extent, Senegal is twenty times as large as The Gambia and its population is ten times as large. In their basic economic structures, however, the two countries have many similarities. Both are largely agricultural export economies that rely heavily on one product – groundnuts. In both countries, the bulk of the population finds employment in the agricultural sector, where production is undertaken, mainly on a traditional basis, partly for subsistence and partly for the market. Senegal's primary product sector has undergone some diversification since 1971, minerals (phosphates) having assumed a substantial importance. Further diversification is in prospect on the basis of iron ore development in eastern Senegal; offshore petroleum deposits have also been located.

During the 1970s, unfavourable prices for their main export crop and drought conditions combined to affect the export earnings of both countries quite severely, but even in normal conditions each country typically records a substantial trade deficit. Geographically the export trade of Senegal is highly concentrated, with a high though diminishing share of its import and export trade – 31 per cent and 36 per cent respectively in 1980 – being undertaken with France. The export trade of The Gambia is less highly concentrated geographically on the import side, about 25 per cent coming from the UK in 1979–80 and 52 per cent from the EEC as a whole. In the same year, about 18 per cent of exports went to the UK, and 72 per cent to the EEC as a whole.

At this point, however, the resemblance ends, for Senegal is not merely a primary product producer. It also possesses the most developed manufacturing sector in francophone Africa after the Ivory Coast. In nominal terms (that is, valuing products at domestic market prices), Senegal's industrial sector generates a share of GDP comparable to that generated by agriculture. Its manufacturing base initially developed when Dakar was the capital of the AOF and its products were able to circulate freely throughout the customs union. Senegal has managed to continue to export its manufactures to several other countries of francophone Africa inside the preferential framework established by CEAO. To a limited extent it also exports to non-preferential markets in the West African region, including The Gambia. During the past decade, Senegal's industries have increasingly experienced acute competition from Ivory Coast, particularly within CEAO, and, partly as a result, its industrial growth has been sluggish. Substantial excess capacity currently exists in a wide range of manufacturing sectors.

In comparison with Senegal, The Gambia's economic structure is less diversified, and its potential for development in purely national terms is more limited. It has no known exploitable mineral resources and it has one of the smallest domestic markets of any African economy. Agriculture generates the bulk of GDP (nearly three-fifths in 1977–8). Groundnuts alone account for 37 per cent of The Gambia's GDP and are the source of the bulk of its domestic exports. Subsistence cropping of millet, sorghum and rice makes up most of the rest of Gambian agricultural output. Agricultural production takes place predominantly on small family farms, and it is heavily dependent on rainfall, the variability of which causes sharp fluctuations in economic activity. The Gambia's industrial base is presently negligible. Apart from a few plants processing groundnuts, small factories producing such products as paint, soap and building materials, and the large modern brewery in Banjul, its industries are basically of an artisanal type.

Despite the inherent limitations of the Gambian economy, its overall economic growth was not unsatisfactory during the 1960s, when an annual average growth rate of 4.5 per cent was achieved against a rate of population growth of only 2.6 per cent. *Per capita* incomes reached a peak of $260 in 1967–8 (in 1976–7 prices), when the impact of growth in groundnut production was reinforced by increased local processing of the product and by good prices. Between 1969 and 1977 severe droughts affected the production of groundnuts and dampened economic performance in general. During this period public administration and tourism were the only sectors to record growth. The average annual growth rate of 1.5 per cent was, moreover, well below the rate of growth of population, and GDP *per capita* declined to about $200 in 1976–7.

The differing economic structures of the two countries have produced markedly different development strategies, which are manifested notably in their respective industrial policies. In Senegal, which possesses a much larger domestic market, an industrial tradition and a rail link to Mali, industrial policy has been directed towards restructuring and developing the initially inherited industrial base to serve both the domestic market and the markets available within the preferential trade groupings, such as the CEAO, that succeeded the AOF. In The Gambia by contrast, the negligible size of the domestic market has discouraged any significant attempt to develop import substitution industries. These differences of approach are reinforced in the case of Senegal by its inability to use the exchange rate as an instrument for maintaining external balance because of its membership of the West African Monetary Union (UMOA).

In Senegal a highly protective trade policy is followed. Import duties are generally very high and rates of 80 and 90 per cent are common. The operation of a system of administrative prices (*valeurs mercuriales*) for certain products in practice enhances the effects of its already high tariff. Imports are also subject to administrative controls and quantitative restrictions. As part of its adjustment policies to deal with current economic difficulties, the Senegalese authorities have extended these controls, and imports from whatever source are closely monitored. In The Gambia by contrast, a liberal trade policy is pursued. Imports may be freely imported from most sources, and licences affect only some 30–35 per cent of trade. Import duties are relatively low. In 1980–1, the height of the tariff as measured by the ratio of duty to the value of imports was about 18 per cent. Many items enter duty-free and rates of duty rarely exceed 25 per cent, except for certain luxury items including motor vehicles, cosmetics and alcoholic beverages.

Partly as a result of these differences in foreign trade policy, there have existed for many years substantial differences in the level and structure of costs and prices in the two countries. Within Senegal, imported goods are relatively expensive because of its high import duties and other restrictions; these high prices effectively set the prices of locally produced import substitutes, many of which are items of mass consumption. In the past, Senegal's membership of the franc zone contributed to the price-level differences. When integration was first discussed two decades ago, the cost and price differences between the two countries were very large. It was estimated at that time that food prices were 100 per cent higher in Dakar than in Banjul, wages 80 per cent higher, and the cost of living about 50 per cent higher. Estimates made in 1982 suggest that the extra cost of buying typical Banjul baskets of commodities in Dakar would now be only 10–20 per cent, depending on whether a traditional or a European pattern of consumption is assumed. Differences in living costs appear therefore to have narrowed during the past two decades. Nevertheless, substantial differences in the prices of individual items continue to exist and there are also important differences in wage and salary levels in the urban sectors.

Trade between the two countries exhibits several special features. First, a large balance of trade is recorded in favour of Senegal; in 1979–80, according to the statistics of The Gambia, this was of the order of 4m. dalasi (£1m.). Second, whereas the bulk of Senegal's exports are domestic in origin, those of The Gambia are mainly re-exports. The Gambia indeed records a flourishing re-export trade not only with neighbouring parts of Senegal, including the Casamance, which it is very well placed to serve, but also with Guinea and Guinea–Bissau, which are the principal outlets (accounting for 65–70 per cent) and with Mali, Mauretania and Sierra Leone. Third,

The Gambia's exports to Senegal are largely unrecorded. The relatively low prices in The Gambia of many imported products in comparison with those in Senegal, together with the impossibility of effectively policing the land frontiers, produce a substantial clandestine export trade. Smuggling also takes place into other countries such as Guinea, Guinea–Bissau and Sierra Leone, where stringent exchange restrictions reinforce the price incentive to trade.

Clandestine trade is of considerable importance to the economy of The Gambia. In the first place the government derives revenue from the embodied import duties (few drawbacks are paid even in respect of recorded re-exports). Secondly, the distributive mark-up accrues to the private sector as income. It is not possible in the nature of the case to estimate the precise significance of the unrecorded re-export trade, but the orders of magnitude can be established by comparing the total imports of The Gambia with independent estimates of private consumption. On this basis it is estimated conservatively that some 25 per cent of recorded imports is destined for re-export. It is further estimated (based on a survey of exported products and prices) that the re-export value of goods includes a profit margin of 11 per cent, which accrues to the trader in The Gambia, and some 27.5 per cent for import duty, which for the most part (drawbacks not being paid) is retained by the Treasury.

It thus appears that in 1979–80 some 20m. dalasi of government revenue was derived directly from recorded and unrecorded re-exports. This represents about 35 per cent of total revenue from import duties and about 25 per cent of total tax revenue. Private income generated by the trade has been put at 8m. dalasi. The re-export trade as a whole (of which perhaps one-third is recorded) has been growing relatively rapidly during the past decade. In 1980–1, when the total value of *domestic* exports was 53m. dalasi, total re-exports may have been in the region of 45–50m. dalasi. In some recent years the value of re-exports is believed to have exceeded the value of domestic exports.

Public revenue from this source is clearly vulnerable. It is sensitive in the first place to The Gambia's own tariff. A significant increase in certain Gambian tariffs could render such trade unprofitable. This has happened already for certain categories of trade such as green tea. But, equally, revenue from this source is vulnerable to changes in tariff policy in neighbouring countries. A case in point is the reduction in the Senegalese tariff on electrical appliances, radios and cassettes that, a few years ago, effectively wiped out the substantial flow of these goods to Senegal through The Gambia.

Unrecorded trade is not without its economic costs to The Gambia, since it creates opportunities to export capital without authorisation and has undoubtedly produced a leakage of foreign exchange. But it is, of course, at the level of its relations with Senegal that the clandestine trade creates most difficulties for The Gambia. Smuggling (carried out, it should be said, principally by traders from Senegal and other neighbouring countries) is a constant irritant and it played a large part in the border troubles of 1969–70. Its revenue importance to The Gambia was a major obstacle to the negotiations on integration two decades ago, since when its importance has substantially increased. Its importance to Senegal is in relative terms much smaller, although it is not negligible. For 1979–80, not more than 70 per cent of the tax revenue estimated to have been raised in The Gambia from re-exports can be attributable to Senegal. That amount – 14m. dalasi, £3.75m. – represents a national income loss to Senegal. If instead, the relevant products had been imported direct into Senegal and taxed at typical Senegal rates – which are of the order of three times the average Gambian tariff – the revenue gain by Senegal would be of the order of 2 per cent of ordinary fiscal revenues.

THE COSTS AND BENEFITS OF ECONOMIC INTEGRATION IN SENEGAMBIA

If, as seems relevant, attention is concentrated initially on the customs union aspects of economic integration in Senegambia, it is apparent that there are two sets of problems: (1) the problems that typically arise in any customs union embracing more advanced and less advanced partners; (2) the unique additional problem that arises from clandestine trade, or unrecorded re-exports, from The Gambia.

If a customs union were established on the basis that The Gambia adjusts its tariffs upwards to those of Senegal, three effects for The Gambia would follow: a substantial amount of trade diversion would take place as Senegalese products replace imports from the rest of the world in The Gambia, involving a corresponding loss of real national income; domestic wages and prices in The Gambia would begin an upward adjustment in the direction of the higher levels of Senegal; and The Gambia would lose a substantial part of its re-export trade – not only its unrecorded trade with Senegal but also its recorded re-export trade with Senegal, with Guinea and with other neighbouring countries, which also depends in part on The Gambia's lower tariff levels. There would be heavy consequential losses of government revenue and of personal income for The Gambia's private traders, both of which would represent corresponding losses of national income. Against these costs must be set increased potential opportunities for The Gambia to export to Senegal; but in practice there are only two industries that would be significantly affected – soap and beer. Any gains would, moreover, be transitional, since once wages and prices had risen in The Gambia there is no reason to expect that these industries would continue to possess any significant cost advantages by comparison with their Senegalese counterparts.

The first and third effects just outlined would, of course, have their counterparts in Senegal, which in its case would be wholly favourable. Senegal would be able to expand its exports to The Gambia substantially, by exporting the products of its fairly well-developed, if high-cost, manufacturing industries, in many of which there exists much excess capacity. From Senegal's viewpoint, this export expansion would be of benefit irrespective of whether it represented trade creation or trade diversion, but for the most part it must represent trade diversion, since apart from beer and soap there are no industries to contract in The Gambia. In addition, Senegal would cease to incur the real income loss that is involved in the clandestine re-export trade.

In short, a simple customs union would be greatly detrimental to The Gambia, from whose point of view indeed it has no conceivable merit. It would be correspondingly advantageous to Senegal.

An alternative approach to integration between the two countries could be founded on the establishment of a free trade area. This would have few if any disadvantages for The Gambia, and indeed would offer the prospect of some significant gains. It would permit a continuance of the recorded and unrecorded re-export trade of The Gambia. It would also provide The Gambia's few import substitution industries with the benefit of import-duty-free access to Senegal's market. This would be important for beer and soap. It could also encourage the establishment of new industries in The Gambia that could only be viable with a larger market. In a free trade area, these important advantages would not be of short duration but should be capable of being maintained for longer periods of time.

There would clearly be an increased penetration of the market of The Gambia for certain products in which Senegalese industry is relatively competitive and has already shown some ability to compete but, by comparison with the customs union, a free trade area would be very much to be preferred by The Gambia and perhaps indeed would even be preferable by comparison with the present situation. But correspondingly it would have few attractions for Senegal. It may not, in any event, be regarded as constituting an acceptable base for meeting the obligations of the Confederation Agreement.

There is a third possibility – first suggested in the UN report of 1964 (Gambia, 1964) and sometimes still mentioned. This would involve a qualified customs union in which Gambia would be permitted as a transitional measure to import quotas of goods at its existing rates of duty. The general quotas would be related to its present levels of apparent consumption and there would be special quotas for sensitive items of importance in the re-export trade. This procedure would cushion The Gambia for the duration of the quotas from the effects of trade diversion and from revenue losses in the re-export trade, and would similarly postpone the rise in domestic costs and prices otherwise to be expected. But of course it would do nothing in the long run to insulate The Gambia from the costs involved in the full customs union.

If the context of economic integration is to be a full customs union, then it is clear that it would only be possible to overcome its prospective disadvantages for The Gambia and for the latter to derive positive benefits if it were to be accompanied by offsetting negotiated benefits for The Gambia in one or more of the following areas: revenue allocation; industrial development; transport and services.

In a simple customs union, revenue allocation is based on attribution. It is however possible for it to be based on revenue-sharing, which implies redistribution. This happens for instance in the Southern African Customs Union, where the shares of Botswana, Lesotho and Swaziland are substantially higher than the duty content of their imports. A similar procedure was followed in the East African Common Market, which preceded the now defunct East African Community. There are precedents for the adoption of other similarly motivated ways of dealing with the costs of trade diversion in West Africa in the practices of CEAO and ECOWAS.

An alternative approach to dealing with an imbalance of costs and benefits in a customs union is through the adoption of a regional industrial allocation system that might assign certain industries to the more backward members, or provide preferential treatment to such industries. Given the magnitude of the prospective losses involved for The Gambia in the establishment of a customs union in Senegambia and the situation of almost universal excess capacity that exists in Senegal's industry, it is difficult to believe that such an arrangement would be easy to negotiate.

There is a third possibility where closer integration might be capable of yielding substantial net gains for the area as a whole out of which benefits to The Gambia could be provided without adversely affecting established interests in Senegal. Opportunities for the optimal use and development of the Senegambian river basin could result in increased agricultural production and the development of certain new agro-industries. It was for this purpose that the Gambia River Development Organisation (OMVG) was established in 1978. A variety of schemes for development is under consideration with aid donors. Impending developments such as the salt barrage could generate important benefits for agricultural development in The Gambia and also better satisfy some of the transport requirements of Senegal by providing easier access to its southern province of Casamance over the proposed combined barrage and road bridge. But it is perhaps in the expanded use of Banjul's port and the Gambia River for meeting some of the expanding external trade requirements of Senegal that most might be gained for The Gambia. A notable instance of possible gains is afforded by the large prospective transport requirements for the evacuation of iron ore from Senegal's eastern province. An unpublished donor study of 1977 *inter alia* compared the cost of evacuating iron ore by the existing Senegalese railway through Dakar (or a nearby port) with the alternative of constructing a spur to deliver the ore from Senegal Oriental to Kuntaur, from which it would be evacuated to Europe and Japan via the Gambia River by smaller ore boats. The study estimated that total annual savings of $28m. could be obtained if this alternative rail/river mode of transport were to be selected. It is likely that some of these prospective gains would materialise only in the context of a customs and economic union, in part because of the long-term commitments that would be involved.

MONETARY ASPECTS OF CONFEDERATION

With respect to the monetary union aspects of confederation, there are broadly three alternatives, of which only the first is capable of being adopted by the bilateral decision of the Senegambian Confederation.

The first option would be for a monetary agreement to be entered into between the governments of The Gambia and Senegal whereby The Gambia would bind itself to maintain the dalasi freely convertible into the CFA franc (which circulates widely in The Gambia already) at an irrevocably fixed rate. This might be termed a *partial monetary union*. An element of uncertainty about the exchange rate must, of course, be present as long as countries issue their own currencies, since it is possible that a country may change its exchange rate. A fixed rate in this context would simply mean that it would be changed only under exceptional circumstances. For The Gambia, such an agreement would mean principally the replacement of the existing sterling link by the franc link, with implications for the trade-weighted value of the dalasi. Certain changes in exchange control would also be implied. The option would have no obvious merits

,for The Gambia over its present freedom to choose among this and other options.

The second option would be for Senegal to withdraw from the West African Monetary Union (UMOA) and to re-enter, together with The Gambia, as Senegambia. In the process, the dalasi would be replaced by the CFA franc. The constitutional and operational implications of such an option for The Gambia are not easy to determine, but the practical significance would substantially depend on specific understandings arrived at between the governments of The Gambia and Senegal with respect to the operation of monetary policy in the combined area and the technical possibilities of differentiating the impact of monetary policy in different parts of the Confederation. This is not an option that could be adopted without the assent of Senegal's partners (Ivory Coast, Upper Volta, Niger, Benin and Togo) in the West African Monetary Union. The assent of France would also be required since, under a Cooperation Agreement with the member states, France underpins the international convertibility of the CFA franc, which is not itself traded on the foreign exchange markets. This option is clearly the one that Senegal, looking to ultimate economic union with The Gambia, can be expected to prefer.

The third option would be for The Gambia to enter the West African Monetary Union as a full member, having a national agency of the Central Bank of West African States (BCEAO) in Banjul that would perform for The Gambia most of the functions now performed by its own central bank. If there is to be a monetary union, this would seem to be the most attractive option from The Gambia's standpoint. It would enjoy an equal voice in the affairs of the Union, and through the National Credit Committee it would have substantial discretion over the details of monetary policy in The Gambia. Its reserves would be pooled with those of other members, but would, in effect, be separately identifiable. The reserves – or the bulk of them – would be kept in Franch francs, but their value would be guaranteed by France in terms of the value of the IMF Special Drawing Right (SDR). The Gambia would be obliged to harmonise its monetary and credit and fiscal policies with those of Senegal, but its growth rate would be determined largely by its own domestic conditions of supply and capital inflows. It would effectively have to operate so that in the long run its external account would be balanced; but, in the short run, access to the pooled reserves of the Union would be possible. This option could be a very attractive one for The Gambia.

There are well-established advantages of monetary union against which, however, macroeconomic costs may have to be set. The experience of the member countries of the UMOA does not suggest that the macro-costs of pursuing the monetary and fiscal policies that are a precondition of membership have been damaging to their performance. But again this is not an option that can be decided on by Senegal and The Gambia alone.

The monetary aspects of a Senegambian economic and monetary union may turn out to be the least troublesome of the issues surrounding the Confederation since there are clearly options that would not adversely affect Senegal's interest or those of her partners, and that could at the same time be beneficial to The Gambia – namely, participation in a wider monetary union of which they are both members. But the absorption of The Gambia into the West African Monetary Union effectively through Senegal's membership would not be in The Gambia's interest. Whichever alternative is pursued, the choice of the rate at which The Gambia would demonetise or stabilise could be crucial.

CONCLUSION

The issue of closer economic cooperation between The Gambia and Senegal has been on the agenda for at least twenty years. Prior to 1981 the view of the Gambian authorities rightly appears to have been that there were serious disadvantages in entering into a form of economic cooperation with its more advanced neighbour that would be limited to a simple customs union. The issue has now to be considered in an entirely different context since a political decision has been made and a Senegambian confederation has been brought into existence, one element of which is 'the development of an economic and monetary union'. It is at the same time clearly intended by President Jawara that the detailed protocols and agreements that are required to implement the Confederation Agreement shall fully safeguard the interests of The Gambia.

The policy problem is to devise arrangements that, while fulfilling The Gambia's obligation to develop an economic and monetary union, make the rate of progress towards those goals conditional on the development of measures of positive economic integration that would promote the interests of both member states. At the same time, any arrangements for a Senegambian economic and monetary union, and more particularly for its customs union aspects, must be constructed in the light of the obligations of both countries towards ECOWAS, which itself aims at the creation of a customs union together with an important range of other measures of economic cooperation. The arrangements adopted for Senegambia must therefore clearly be consistent with present ECOWAS obligations, or

there must at least be a prospect of their being subsequently legitim-
ised, if they are to endure beyond the second phase of development
of ECOWAS.

With respect to the timing of the introduction of a common external tariff with Senegal, this could not be delayed beyond the third
phase of the ECOWAS timetable. However, the standstill agreement
of ECOWAS presumably also rules out any earlier upward revision
of The Gambia's tariff. Consequently, tariff harmonisation with
Senegal would either have to take place by an all-round lowering of
the Senegal tariff, which is inconceivable, or it would have to await
the eventual adoption by both countries of the common external
tariff of ECOWAS according to the latter's timetable.

Subject to this constraint, it would not be difficult to devise
arrangements for accelerated trade liberalisation in the context of a
confederal customs union agreement that would preserve the interest
of The Gambia during this period. This could be done by making the
pace of trade liberalisation conditional on expanded export opportunities for The Gambia in Senegal, or alternatively by requiring the
payment of fiscal compensation by Senegal in respect of any revenue
losses incurred by The Gambia as a result of accelerated trade liberalisation. Given the obligations imposed by ECOWAS, such an
arrangement would formally have to be regarded as transitional,
although the period during which it could operate, being conditional
on the prospects of ECOWAS, might well be fairly lengthy.

In the longer run, however, with or without confederation, the
existence of ECOWAS obligations will make it difficult, if not
impossible, to preserve the interests of The Gambia with respect to
Senegal, for the provisions of the Treaty of Lagos that are designed to
protect the interest of less developed members of the Community
against industrially more advanced members are inadequate. The
Treaty of Lagos does provide for fiscal compensation for revenue
losses incurred during the process of trade liberalisation, but compensation for losses arising from trade creation is not envisaged. More
important in the context of Senegambia, the ECOWAS measures to
promote balanced development are not linked closely to the creation
of the common external tariff and trade liberalisation, but are dependent on the operation of mechanisms yet to be introduced and whose
efficacy is as yet unproven. The interests of The Gambia with respect
to Senegal can only be assured if The Gambia and other less
developed members of ECOWAS successfully press for improved
safeguards for the less advanced members of ECOWAS in the context of that grouping. In such a context, transitional preferential
arrangements that might conceivably be acceptable to both parties in
a Senegambian Confederation might also be tolerated as more per-

manent features of intra-Community relations; or, if appropriate alternative policies were developed by ECOWAS itself, they might be allowed to lapse and be replaced by the latter.

Unless such improved arrangements relieve the less developed members of the obligation to adopt a common external tariff – permitting them in effect to operate a free trade area tier within the Community – a loss of real income from curtailed re-export trade would ultimately be unavoidable for The Gambia. That would face the Gambian authorities with the unpleasant choice between either trying to maintain their by no means extravagant standard of public services by substantially increasing the tax burden on consumers and enterprises, or instead cutting back the level of public services in order to maintain a roughly constant tax effort. The choice would be an unenviable one.

8 Monetary Cooperation and West African Integration

The monetary and exchange regimes that underly the three West African integration arrangements are extremely varied. In ECOWAS, exchange regimes range from virtually complete convertibility in Liberia to complete inconvertibility in Ghana. Within CEAO, four members are part of a wider monetary union that is linked to the French franc; a fifth member – Mali – has a currency that is similarly pegged to the French franc. In the Mano River Union, the currencies of Sierra Leone and Guinea are inconvertible, while that of Liberia is largely convertible. What are the implications of this diversity for economic integration in West Africa? Is monetary integration necessary to give effect to the integration of product markets? Is it feasible? If not, are alternative arrangements for monetary cooperation possible that can provide some of the benefits of monetary integration? Has monetary integration involved macroeconomic costs for the members of the West African Monetary Union in terms of their relative economic performance? This chapter first analyses some of the monetary issues and problems that arise in connection with integration, and that bear on these questions. It then reviews in turn the experiences of the West African Monetary Union and of the West African Clearing House. There is an awareness in West Africa that monetary problems need early resolution if they are not to frustrate regional economic integration. At the twelfth Meeting of the Committee of West African Central Banks in 1981 the problems of currency inconvertibility were once again considered, the Committee having previously received an IMF report on the subject (BCEAO, 1982b).

THE SIGNIFICANCE OF MONETARY INTEGRATION

Full monetary integration implies two conditions: (1) an exchange rate union, which requires that exchange rates in the area bear a permanently fixed relationship to each other; (2) convertibility, in the sense of a permanent absence of exchange controls in respect of both current and capital transactions within the area. Convertibility for trade-related transactions is indispensable for an effective customs union. The additional element of convertibility involved in monetary integration is capital market integration. This entails the establishment of a unified capital market free from geographical restrictions of any kind on capital movements. Capital market integration is a requirement of a common market.

Monetary integration in the sense defined requires the unification and joint management of both monetary policy and the external exchange rate policy of the union. This in turn entails further consequences. First, in the monetary field, the rate of increase of the money supply must be decided jointly. Beyond an agreed amount of credit expansion allocated to each member state's central bank, a member state must finance any budget deficit in the union's capital market at the ruling rate of interest. A unified monetary policy would remove one of the main reasons for disparate movements in members' price levels. Secondly, the balance of payments of the entire union with the rest of the world must be regulated at union level. For this purpose, the monetary authority must dispose of the common pool of exchange reserves, and the exchange rate of the union with other currencies must be regulated at the union level. Under such a system, it may not be possible for a member to calculate its balance of payments with its partners and the rest of the world.

Monetary integration offers the prospect of important benefits. The first advantage rests on its impact on resource allocation, which it is the central purpose of economic integration to improve. This has two dimensions. Monetary integration guarantees, in the most convincing way open to countries that retain their separate national identities and political sovereignty, that currency restrictions will never hinder trade between the member countries. The availability of convertible currency is clearly a basic requirement for effective market integration and for securing the initial advantages of free trade amongst the members of the group that are determined largely by the existing production structures. Monetary integration also encourages the changes in investment allocation in the combined market that are required to secure the full static gains from integration. These gains are derived from the impact of integration on the production structures themselves by way of changes in the scale and techniques of production and its geographical distribution. These changes should raise incomes and, if accompanied by a rise in the rate of investment in the region, they should produce an accelerated growth rate. But since investment decisions are long run in nature, these further effects will be felt only to the extent that entrepreneurs can confidently assume that a combined market will be maintained and that profits can be repatriated. In the presence of separate states, this confidence can best be engendered – perhaps can only be engendered – by the establishment of a common currency and a monetary union.

A second source of gain may be secured from economies in the use of foreign exchange reserves. When a common currency is established and a common pool of foreign exchange is created, the quantity of reserves required may be reduced for two reasons: since members with different export bases are unlikely to experience similar payments fluctuations at the same times, a pooling of reserves will economise them, so long as the formation of the monetary union does not itself increase economic fluctuations; and foreign exchange will no longer be needed to finance intra-union trade.

Reduced costs of financial management provide a third source of gain. Integration should make it possible to spread the overhead costs of financial transactions more widely and, in addition, some part of the activities of foreign exchange dealing institutions could be dispensed with, thus generating resource-use savings.

A full monetary union clearly imposes constraints on the use of certain economic policy instruments on the part of its members, and this may entail real economic costs. The costs are at a minimum when a variety of conditions are satisfied, which economists have attempted to embody in the concept of optimum currency areas.

Full monetary integration is evidently not on the immediate agenda of West African integration, and rightly so. Whether the region is looked at in terms of orthodox criteria for the delineation of optimal currency areas (Ishiyama, 1975; Nana-Sinkam, 1978) or broader criteria (Robson, 1980), it appears to lack the characteristics suitable for monetary union; nor is it likely to acquire them soon. In particular, the member countries conduct the bulk of their trade with third countries and have markedly different export patterns. Changes in their export receipts are not correlated, and diversity in their trends would require disparate changes in exchange rates, quite apart from inter-country differences in rates of monetary expansion.

Full monetary integration is not, however, a prerequisite for market integration, although it might be a necessary condition for maximising the potential static and dynamic resource allocation gains. Even the EEC lacks a common currency. But, equally clearly, some elements of monetary cooperation and harmonisation are necessary if market integration is not to be frustrated. Even its first stage – trade liberalisation – may have far-reaching implications for the harmonisation of monetary and exchange rate policies. Beyond this, it may be possible, by the appropriate development of institutions, to secure at least some of the subsidiary gains associated with monetary integration without going as far as the adoption of common currencies.

The Monetary Requirements of an Economic Community

The basic monetary requirement of an effective customs union or an economic community is that there should be current intra-regional convertibility – that is, an absence of exchange controls in respect of current trade-related exchange transactions within the group. If this requirement does not exist, the incidence of trade liberalisation will, at the very least, be modified and could even, in the limiting case, be completely nullified. Thus, unless one type of economic barrier (tariffs) is to be replaced by another (exchange controls), convertibility is a prerequisite. In the West African region, convertibility does not exist, except for and within the West African Monetary Union and, effectively, for Liberia. Its importance is nevertheless clearly recognised in the Lagos Treaty, and studies are under way by ECOWAS, under the auspices of the Committee of Central Banks, with a view to arriving at a partial convertibility.

The convertibility requirement evidently has far-reaching implications. The seriousness of these will depend on the degree of currency overvaluation that will be denoted by the severity of the exchange restrictions. Even if trade liberalisation is introduced initially without the adoption of a common tariff, in the presence of overvaluations disequilibria may be created that may force exchange rate adjustments. The eventual adoption of a common external tariff when trade liberalisation is complete (as envisaged in ECOWAS), will have further implications for the respective exchange rates of member countries. ECOWAS countries will not be able to avoid this problem by applying diverse national exchange controls to transactions with the rest of the world while dismantling their exchange restrictions on current intra-Community transactions.

Although not all West African countries have overvalued exchange rates, overvaluation is common, and in some cases severe (African Centre for Monetary Studies, 1979; World Bank, 1981b). Some of the problems this would otherwise present when a full customs union is attained will be avoided by specific provisions of the respective treaties of integration. For instance, in ECOWAS the transfer of goods imported from third countries to other member states is subject to control. The same is true of the Mano River Union. Thus importers would be prevented from circumventing stringent exchange controls directed against the outside world by indirectly importing through a more liberal partner – form of 'monetary' trade deflection. Nevertheless, since current account convertibility would exclude exchange restrictions on imports of Community origin from other countries, it would still be possible, at a price, for the varying severity of exchange controls in a grouping to be partly circumvented – for smaller countries with severe restrictions perhaps completely – by *indirect* trade deflection stimulated by exchange control differences rather than, as in the orthodox case (Robson, 1980) by tariff differences. The intra-group trade imbalances so created would, in the absence of special arrangements, have to be settled in convertible currencies. As to capital convertibility, the considerations are rather different, but this aspect will be disregarded.

Fixed or Flexible Intra-Community Exchange Rates?

The first condition of full monetary integration noted above is that exchange rates should be fixed within the group. If monetary union does not accompany economic and market integration it has nevertheless to be considered whether it is necessary or desirable that exchange rates should be stable amongst the members of economic groupings. Should rates be pegged, and if so within what range, or should they be free to float? The question is concerned not with the general implications of fixed or floating rates for developing countries, but with the specific implications of the two alternatives for the process of economic integration. From this narrower point of view, the answer must depend on the effects of the two alternatives upon the relative prices of an integrating country's products with respect to those of its partners. The prices of goods exported to the rest of the world under competitive conditions may not be significantly affected by the alternative chosen. However, the manufactured products that constitute the major ingredient of intra-group trade in integration among developing countries typically have sticky prices and fixed costs. Fixed rates of exchange would keep the sticky prices stable among the integrating countries, whereas floating rates would alter their relationships with respect to substitutes from partner countries and from third countries. Fluctuations of relative prices, so the orthodox argument runs, will severely hinder the growth of intra-regional trade in imperfect markets.

Where different rates of inflation coexist among the members of the group, the relevant consideration is not variations in the nominal parity rate but rather variations in the 'real' rate of exchange, defined as the index of the exchange rate to that of domestic prices. Changes in this rate will denote changes in the international competitiveness of domestic products that result from disparate movements in domestic prices and exchange parities. Fluctuations in the real exchange rate create uncertainty in foreign trade and will tend to discriminate against exporting activities. With fixed exchange rates the real rate must be expected to fluctuate, since increases in domestic prices are normally continuous while changes in parities take place discontinuously. This is clearly likely to create difficulties, since, although a producer can usually raise prices in domestic markets to reflect his increased costs, this possibility will not be open to him in the other markets of the group. Thus his receipts in terms of domestic currency will depend on the stage of the inflation–devaluation cycle reached at the time his sales proceeds are repatriated. Fluctuations in the real exchange rate could therefore create distortionary shifts in the pattern of intra-group trade, as the experience of Latin American integration shows (Krueger, 1969, p. 169). If these fluctuations are severe, any likely benefits from market integration might be far outweighed by the costs of resource misallocation. It is hard to see how resources can be allocated efficiently in the group if sudden changes in relative real rates occur frequently. To the extent that floating rates can avoid these problems, the adoption of such a system might be regarded as advantageous in the context of integration.

Although it is valid to conclude that in principle it is desirable for fluctuations in real exchange rates to be avoided amongst the members of an economic grouping, it is by no means clear that floating rates will eliminate such fluctuations, although they should reduce them. In any event, the conclusion is of no policy relevance in the context of integration in West Africa, since the institutional features of the underdeveloped exchange and financial markets of the West African countries coupled with their trading patterns clearly rule out floating as an optimal policy in the foreseeable future. The considerations have been well set out by Black (1976). West African currencies will no doubt, for well-understood reasons, remain pegged. The only important question concerns the choice of the peg.

But if the evidently important monetary obstacles to economic integration are to be overcome, certain monetary changes would be essential. In the first place, exchange rate realignments will certainly be initially necessary to reduce the more severe elements of overvaluation that exist within the region, and to make regional convertibility feasible in the context of trade liberalisation; the abolition of quantitative restrictions, and the adoption of a common external tariff. Thereafter, if priority is attached to the monetary requirements of integration, monetary expansion in each country will have to be limited to what is consistent with the maintenance of overall external balance, given the level of the common external tariff and regional free trade. That would imply a substantial degree of *de facto* harmonisation of monetary policies, and it would, of course, largely overcome the problem of fluctuating real-rates of exchange.

Broader Areas For Monetary Cooperation

Beyond this there are certain other areas where monetary cooperation measures may be important for the progress of economic integration, or desirable as a means of securing the benefits associated with monetary integration. The three principal areas are: credit agreements; payments arrangements; and reserve pooling.

It is possible that certain members of the group may experience temporary balance of payments problems as a direct result of trade liberalisation and the adoption of a common external tariff, while, at the same time, these measures deprive them of policy instruments for coping with such difficulties. Fear of such difficulties appears to be one of the main deterrents to the implementation of trade liberalisation obligations in economic groupings. In these circumstances, the provision of automatic credits to finance balance of payments difficulties arising from regional integration could then be desirable pending the necessary exchange rate adjustments and resource reallocation. Operational criteria would clearly have to be worked out for determining what part of any balance of payments deterioration results from integration. It has been argued (Cooper, 1969, pp. 164–5) that credits for this purpose should be financed by those countries whose intra-regional balance of payments improves, on the ground that such an improvement would reflect the relative advantages that those countries would enjoy from integration. This would be one way of distributing the benefits from integration. Many problems are involved in the issue of who should supply the reserves to finance such deficits however (Robson, 1968), and it is not clear that the adoption of intra-regional balance of trade or payments criteria for determining the borrowing or lending obligations of member countries would operate satisfactorily.

An important advantage of a monetary union is that it eliminates the cost of foreign exchange dealing with respect to intra-union transactions. It may be possible for an economic grouping to obtain this gain without establishing a monetary union by setting up a clearing union or a clearing house through which payments among the members would be directly channelled instead of going through traditional financial centres outside the region. This procedure could reduce exchange transaction costs by limiting the need for convertible currencies (on the basis of which intra-group trade would otherwise be conducted) to the *net* balance of any country with the group. Whether any real economies would be effected by such a development would depend on the extent to which any economies in the use of foreign currencies would be offset by the administrative costs of operating such an institution.

A third form of cooperation that might enable subsidiary advantages of monetary integration to be secured would be the institution of a limited form of reserve pooling, which could reduce the size of reserves that needed to be held in relation to the group's overall trading positions. It is clear that the terms of trade of individual West African countries fluctuate more widely than those of the group as a whole. It also appears that differences in the export patterns of different countries give rise to divergent changes in foreign exchange receipts. To the extent that fluctuations in export volumes and in the terms of trade are not synchronised, a reserve pooling system could offer some advantages to the group.

The actual post-independence experience of monetary cooperation in West Africa up to the present time centres largely on two institutions, namely, the long-established West African Monetary Union and the more recently established West African Clearing House. A brief account of their operations and experience will serve to highlight some of the issues and problems touched on here and, perhaps, the possibilities of further advances in the monetary arena.

THE WEST AFRICAN MONETARY UNION

The West African Monetary Union (UMOA), which at present comprises six West African countries (Benin, Ivory Coast, Niger, Senegal, Togo and Upper Volta), is an important case of monetary integration whose experience provides significant lessons for West Africa. For twenty years its members have enjoyed a freely circulating common currency, issued by the common central bank, the Banque Centrale des Etats de l'Afrique de l'Ouest (BCEAO). The common currency, the CFA franc, is pegged to the French franc at a rate (1 Ffr. = 50 CFA fr.) that has remained unchanged for thirty-five years. France, which is represented on the Bank's Board of Directors, underpins an unlimited convertibility of the CFA franc into French francs through the mechanism of an operations account with the French Treasury. The foreign exchange reserves of member countries are held by the Central Bank in a common pool, which is deposited in the operations account through which the Bank's foreign exchange operations are conducted.

The statutes of the BCEAO remained virtually unchanged from its establishment in November 1962 until the end of 1974, when substantial modifications were made to empower the bank to influence monetary developments more actively as an instrument of economic development of member countries and to encourage their regional integration. The changes marked the passage from a passive, highly centralised central bank to a more active, decentralised and Africanised bank. The essential features of the previous arrangements – namely, the issue of a common currency, the pooling of external reserves and the convertibility of the CFA franc into the French franc – all continue under the revised regime.

The changes in the monetary union and in the bank's statutes and operations are a response to the marked changes in the political and economic conditions of the member countries that took place over the Bank's first decade. When the BCEAO was established in 1962, all of its member countries were heavily dependent upon France. Most of their primary product exports were sold to France under arrangements that guaranteed prices that were above world market prices. More than two-thirds of their imports originated in France, which was also the major source of their official capital inflows. Since that time there has been a steady lessening of their dependence on France, although it still remains significant, reflecting in part the liberalisation of French exchange policy itself, which, since 1967, has not operated protectively (Guillaumont, 1981). All of the member states have become members of the International Monetary Fund and of the World Bank. They have become associated with the European Economic Community under the conventions of Yaoundé and Lomé. These developments have considerably increased their exposure to finance, trade and investment linkages with countries outside the franc zone, and have given them access to the resources of the international financial institutions. Simultaneously, the economies of the member states have evolved considerably over the period, and their economic policies have become increasingly development-oriented. The pursuit of developmental objectives has typically been reflected in growing budgetary pressures. As a result, the problem of integrating fiscal with monetary policies has increasingly been posed.

The Organisation and Monetary Policy of the BCEAO Prior to 1974

Prior to 1974 the BCEAO had its headquarters in Paris but maintained national agencies in each member country. Formally the Bank was controlled by a Council of Ministers, made up of the ministers of finance of each member state, but management was effectively in the hands of an executive Board of Directors consisting of two directors from each member state and an equal number (that is, twelve in all) from France. Credit and monetary decisions taken by the Board were implemented in each country by a five-man National Monetary Committee appointed by member states and including the two national executive directors of the BCEAO. Day-to-day operations at the national level were the responsibility of the national agencies of the BCEAO, which were headed by national directors. The Bank was not charged with specific responsibilities for maintaining monetary and price stability and balance of payments equilibrium; its operations were to be directed towards maintaining its liquidity. For this purpose the Bank was required to introduce corrective measures once the ratio of average gross foreign assets to average demand liabilities fell below a prescribed level. The overall balance of payments situation was presumably thought to be adequately controllable by limiting the creation of additional liquidity through restricting the credit operations of the Central Bank. All the important decisions of monetary policy (discount ceilings and rate) required a two-thirds majority of the Council, while a majority of three-quarters was required to modify the obligatory corrective measures imposed when the ratio of foreign assets to demand liabilities fell below 10 per cent.

Instruments of monetary control at the disposition of the BCEAO included the authority to fix the rediscount ceilings that ultimately govern central bank credit to commercial banks and to vary the rediscount rate. In addition the commercial banks were compelled to maintain a specified liquidity ratio.

The statutes of the BCEAO imposed a strict limit on its provision of credit to governments. Initially this limit was set at 10 per cent of the fiscal receipts of the previous year, but it was later raised to 15 per cent. For this purpose, credit to government includes direct advances to the governments by the BCEAO, the holdings of Treasury bills by the BCEAO and the indebtedness of the treasuries towards bank and non-bank financial institutions using BCEAO's rediscount facilities.

During the decade prior to the reforms of 1974, the Central Bank's principal instrument of monetary intervention was not the rediscount ceilings, which remained ineffective (actual rediscounts being well below the ceilings), but the individual commercial credit limits fixed for enterprises in the light of their activities and financial situations and which, by virtue of that fact, became eligible for rediscount at the Central Bank. The object of this policy was to ensure that such rediscountable credits were only accorded to well-managed and solvent enterprises, and, in particular, those having sufficient financial resources of their own. A high proportion of the larger enterprises of the member countries were and are foreign owned, and it was desired by this procedure to prevent the substitution of cheap BCEAO finance for self-finance through undistributed profits or the importation of capital from abroad. Rediscountable credits together with cash constituted the liquidity of the banks for the purpose of calculating their liquidity ratios. The level of interest applicable to rediscountable credit was lower than that applied to non-rediscountable credits.

Throughout the decade 1963–73 the rediscount rate remained at 3.5 per cent.

The increase in liquidity that accompanied this policy did not give rise to problems for the greater part of the decade. For much of the period the overall balance of payments of the Union remained in credit and external assets remained above the minimum prescribed level. The annual rate of domestic price increase in the different member states also remained well below 5 per cent. By the beginning of the 1970s these favourable factors had begun to change. Inflation accelerated. Net foreign assets underwent a sharp decline. There was an excessive increase in non-rediscountable credits, which were accorded by the commercial banks from increased resources that doubtless reflected their foreign borrowing and were outside the control of the Central Bank. Despite the rise in the nominal interest rate in 1973, real rates become negative. Credit expansion became apparently uncontrollable. Whereas, in 1967, the level of liquidity in the UMOA (money supply/gross domestic product) was 14 per cent, ten years later it was 28 per cent (Guillaumont, 1981, p. 15). In 1972, the ratio of external reserves to sight obligations was 71 per cent. By 1974 it was less than 40 per cent. It was to drop further to 24 per cent by 1979 (p. 57).

It is not altogether clear that this outcome was unavoidable within the system as it then existed. It would have been possible for the authorities to raise the rate of interest, to modify the definition of the liquidity coefficient and to establish a system of compulsory reserves without overturning the established instruments of monetary control. But by this time reform on other grounds had in any case become desirable, if not imperative, and quite far-reaching changes followed.

The 1974 Reform of the Monetary Union and Central Bank

The treaty regulating the West African Monetary Union was revised in 1973 and its new provisions came into effect in October 1974. Simultaneously the statutes of the BCEAO were also revised. Subsequently, in 1975, the Council of Ministers approved a substantial revision of the rules of intervention of the BCEAO, providing it with a more comprehensive armoury of monetary instruments than was available under the previous statutes.

The reform of 1974 was prompted by a growing perception of the inadequacy of the previous system and practices for meeting the policy objectives of the member countries of the Union. The conduct of monetary policy during the earlier period suffered from a lack of definition of objectives and this, coupled with constraints on the instruments available, rendered the authorities increasingly unable to

exercise a quantitative or a qualitative control over credit developments. Furthermore, it was felt that the Monetary Union was not
providing an adequate developmental impetus to the development
of the region as a whole. To overcome these limitations, the 1974
reform redefined the objectives of the Bank and revised its monetary
policy instruments as well as its institutional and administrative
structure.

The main features of the reform include: the creation of the Conference of Heads of State as the supreme political body of the Union,
with the Council of Ministers retaining its previous role of direction;
the overhaul of the policy instruments; the decentralisation of powers
so as to provide more autonomy to National Credit Committees (the
successors to the National Monetary Committees) in the field of
credit policy; the transfer of the Bank's central administrative office
from Paris to Dakar; rapid Africanisation of the bank staff; a revision
of the arrangements for monetary cooperation with France; a reduction in the representation of France on the Board. The major organ-
isational change concerns the composition of the Board of Directors.
Under the previous arrangement, France played a predominant role
in the decision-taking of the Bank; its representation on the Board
amounted to one-half of the total, and most decisions required a
two-thirds majority. Under the revised statutes, each member country together with France nominates two directors. The Board takes
some decisions – for example, on the interest rate – by a simple
majority. Certain other important decisions of monetary policy
require a qualified majority. To modify the exchange rate – which is a
matter for the Council of Ministers – unanimity is required.

The new treaty of UMOA explicitly assigns important economic
and financial objectives to the Union. Monetary policy is ascribed an
essential role in the promotion of rapid economic growth and the
harmonisation of the economies of member countries. Other specific
objectives include the protection of the common foreign exchange
reserves and the promotion of price stability. The developmental and
integrational interest attached by the member states to money and
banking was emphasised by the simultaneous creation of a West African Development Bank. Half of its initial capital of 2.4b. fr. CFA is
provided by the BCEAO and the balance by the member states. The
developmental role of the BCEAO itself was further emphasised by
changes in the rules governing its lending to member governments.
The upper limit for advances by the Central Bank to national
treasuries was raised from 15 per cent to 20 per cent of the previous
year's fiscal receipts. In addition, within this limit the Bank may
directly discount government securities with a maturity date of up to
ten years to finance development operations. This provision may

facilitate the co-financing of certain development projects with international organisations.

Under the new Cooperation Agreement, France again agrees to provide support to the West African Monetary Union to ensure free convertibility of the CFA franc. Assistance for this purpose, if and when required, is to be provided mainly in the form of overdraft facilities through the operations account that the BCEAO maintains, as before, with the French Treasury. The new agreement allows some diversification of the BCEAO's foreign reserves: henceforward the BCEAO need maintain only 65 per cent of its foreign currency reserves in French francs as deposits in the operations account with the French Treasury. France guarantees the value of these deposits in terms of the SDR. The exchange value of the CFA franc remains unchanged.

The new statutes and the accompanying rules of intervention provide the BCEAO with a range of policy instruments designed to control both the quantity of credit and its sectoral distribution.

The most important changes relate to the rediscount instrument. Under the new statute individual bank rediscount ceilings were abolished, rediscounting was limited to 35 per cent of any bank's outstanding credits, the automatic access of banks to rediscounting was discontinued, and the distinction between rediscountable and non-rediscountable credit was abolished. In addition, the Bank was empowered to impose reserve requirements on the banks, expressed either as a percentage of their deposits or as a percentage of the credit extended to them. An intra-Union money market was also established, designed to channel funds among member countries.

Rediscount facilities continue to constitute the principal means of Central Bank control over the liquidity of member countries, but the context of its operation was made potentially more positive. The Bank is required to set annual targets of total Central Bank financing in each member state taking into account the evolution of production, prices, the liquidity situation and the balance of payments target as well as the level of external reserves of each country and the total external reserves of the area as a whole. Corrective measures have to be considered once the level of gross external reserves falls below 20 per cent of sight liabilities, but the Board is not obliged automatically to introduce any specific restrictive monetary measure, like the formerly obligatory and automatic reduction in rediscount ceilings.

One of the most important innovations is that the Central Bank's financing limits as determined under the new rules henceforward include credit extended to governments. The overall financing limits for a country are decided by the Board of Directors, but the allocation of the limit between a government and that country's financial institutions is left to the National Credit Committees. Within the prescribed limits for advances by the Central Bank to the national exchequers, it is in practice difficult for credit requests to be refused if a member state is in serious financial difficulties. Consequently the residual financing available for national financial institutions within the national ceiling varies inversely with the requirements of national treasuries. To this limited extent it can be said that under the new regime fiscal policy is coordinated with overall monetary policy.

A further important feature of the new rules is that an active role for interest rate policy is envisaged: interest rates are to be higher (they were sometimes negative in real terms previously) and more flexible.

The new rules also provide the BCEAO with a variety of instruments to influence the sectoral distribution of credit. The most important of these is the requirement for prior authorisation. The commercial banks are required to obtain prior authorisation from the Central Bank for all credit to be accorded beyond a prescribed limit to any single enterprise. The approval procedure is exercised by the National Credit Committees. Its ostensible purpose is to influence the distribution of credit, but it may also be an instrument for influencing overall credit expansion. In addition to this measure and concomitantly with the move towards a more active interest rate policy, the BCEAO is also empowered to institute preferential interest rates for certain kinds of credit (rediscount rates) including loans to small- and medium-sized enterprises and small loans for housing construction.

Monetary Policy in the West African Monetary Union since 1974

Under the new statutes and rules of intervention the BCEAO clearly has a strengthened and better-defined role in monetary policy and an enhanced range of monetary instruments for meeting its objectives. In particular, the Central Bank is accorded the possibility of operating discretionary policies with respect to individual member states. The BCEAO has nevertheless continued until recently to rely mainly on its rediscount facilities to influence overall monetary developments and on the mechanism of prior authorisation to influence the sectoral allocation of credit. More recently, the difficulty of attaining its targets by the exclusive use of the rediscount instrument has led it to introduce a system of monthly overall credit ceilings for certain countries, as well as to revert to ceilings for individual banks.

The new policy has involved more decentralisation of monetary decisions to the level of the states through an enhancement of the role of the National Credit Committees. The rediscounting facilities of each bank within the global total is decided on their advice, and the sectoral distribution of credits is within their exclusive competence. This increased flexibility at the national level has apparently not been accomplished without a certain slippage at the level of global control, which has led to a resort to informal advisory procedures involving the governor of the BCEAO. Nevertheless, under the new system, within the overall orientation of the Union's monetary policy and exchange policy and the general uniformity of its interest rate structure, the national monetary authorities are more able to adopt policies that are appropriate to their national situations.

The more recent imposition of credit ceilings on an aggregate country basis and on individual banks usefully complements the rediscount mechanism as the principal policy instrument. The defect of the rediscount instrument is that it is effective only when commercial banks are compelled to resort to Central Bank financing. In the BCEAO countries the proportion of domestic sector credit refinanced by the BCEAO amounted to only 25 per cent during the period 1977–80, and for ordinary credit (as opposed to seasonal credit for crop financing) the proportion is below 20 per cent, underlining the limited efficacy of the Central Bank's rediscount mechanism for attaining national targets in respect of either credit or external reserves when the commercial banks can resort to other (particularly foreign) sources of financing to supplement domestic deposits, rediscounts, and their operations in the newly created Union money market, in order to meet the demand for credit.

It is difficult to judge the efficacy of the post-reform monetary policies, since the period has been marked by international crisis, worldwide inflation and the emergence of rising deficits generally among the non-oil-producing countries. The gross external reserves of the BCEAO declined from 192,500m. fr. CFA in mid-1977 to 27,400m. fr. CFA in September 1980. The critical level of 20 per cent of reserves to sight liabilities was reached in January 1980 and there was a continuous decline to 6 per cent in September of that year. The seriousness of the deteriorating external position subsequently led to corrective policies being applied throughout the Union, in conjunction with financial assistance provided by the IMF. The effectiveness of these measures has yet to be thoroughly established, but it seems clear that the growth of the monetary aggregates has slowed down since 1980, and that this is in part attributable to the actions of the monetary authorities.

Fiscal Policy Issues in the Monetary Union

A monetary union involving, as it does, an explicit coordination of monetary and exchange policies clearly demands some harmonisation of the fiscal policies of member countries. Without this, unduly divergent national fiscal policies could lead to insupportable stresses within a monetary union through their impact on the balance of payments of the Union and its external reserves, unless the financial consequences of divergence are offset by external inflows of capital into the countries operating the relatively expansionary policies.

In the case of the West African Monetary Union, the principal formal means of fiscal coordination is the statutory limit on credit accorded to member governments by the central banking system. As already noted, the limit in BCEAO is 20 per cent of the previous year's government domestic tax revenue. This amount was originally intended to provide short-term ways and means financing for budgetary operations. The limit refers to the total gross credit outstanding at any point in time and not to a yearly increment in financing.

In addition to the formal limitation on credit, coordination of fiscal policy is further attempted in the process of determining annual monetary targets. Since 1974, the BCEAO determines overall credit targets for each member country that include in each case any credit to be extended to government. In the course of this process, which is subject to the approval of the Council of Ministers, national fiscal requirements are explicitly discussed and considered by the ministers.

The efficacy of the formal limit on bank credit to member governments as a means of inducing fiscal coordination is perhaps debatable (Bhatia, 1982). In practice, the discipline imposed by such a limit can be circumvented in the short run by other means, with undersirable monetary consequences for the Union. For instance, although the Central Bank's credit to governments is limited, increased budgetary deficits may still be financed by external borrowing, by increasing payments arrears and even by the use of various deposits with the treasuries, which themselves perform certain banking functions in some of the member countries. Also, to the extent that there are no statutory limits on credits to the private sector, it may be possible for governments to divert certain budgetary expenditures such as consumer subsidies to public enterprises, which then borrow from the banking system to finance their increased expenditures. Finally, from year to year the member countries may be able to draw down their own bank deposits. It is clear, therefore, that the member states of the Monetary Union have a number of means at their disposal for avoiding, in the short run, the limitations on their fiscal policies that are imposed in principle by the statutes of the Central Bank. In practice, most UMOA member states engage in expansionary fiscal policies that are reflected in their sometimes considerable budget deficits. For the most part, these deficits have been financed by resort to net foreign borrowing, which generates a growing burden of external debt service.

Policy Constraints and Policy Performance in the West African Monetary Union

Monetary union not only involves benefits but, if it imposes offsetting constraints on the growth of output and employment in the member countries, it will also involve costs. The macroeconomic factors that may have to be taken into account from this point of view cannot be discussed here, but are considered at length in Robson (1980). In addition to these factors, the possible costs of having to resort to second-best policy measures, because of the inability of member states in a monetary union to use the exchange rate instrument and possibly, interest rate variations, must also be taken into account.

In the West African Monetary Union there is no formal bar to a change of parity by all members, but it requires unanimity on the part of all, which, given very diverse national positions, is improbable. In practice, any suggestions for parity changes tend to be ill received, and a member country wishing to devalue can therefore only do so by leaving the Monetary Union.

What exactly are the basic constraints imposed by the West African Monetary Union upon its members? These can best be appreciated by recognising the rather special character of the Union, which has succeeded in allowing each country a substantial degree of flexibility in monetary matters while at the same time providing, ultimately, a fairly automatic discipline. In effect, the arrangements subject each member to virtually the same constraints as if each operated its own currency system with a pegged rate.

This is achieved by operating separate accounts of external and other assets and liabilities for each country in the books of the Central Bank. This involves, in the first instance, identifying the note issue in each country separately, although not in a manner that entails any restriction upon the interchangeability of notes within the Union. However, notes issued on one country are withdrawn from circulation when they reach commercial banks in another country and they are returned to the national agencies of the BCEAO in the country of issue. Payments through banks between the member states and between any one of them and the rest of the world through France can also, for the most part, be readily identified. Thus, disregarding clandestine trade, it is possible to arrive from the monetary side at a balance of payments for each country that shows the net effect of the overseas commercial balance, the inflow and outflow of capital, and the balance of intra-Union exchanges. It is then possible to ascribe to any country the responsibility for a change in the jointly held but seperately identified external reserves, whose level in relation to sight liabilities is ultimately critical for monetary policy. Although the BCEAO has only one operations account with the French Treasury, it effectively operates individual operations accounts for each member country. The Union is thus required to operate so that, in the long run, credit expansion within each country is kept within the limits necessary to maintain balance in the individual balance of payments accounts. So long as this is done, short-term variations in each country's reserve position are permissible, and do indeed occur on a substantial scale.

The UMOA system clearly places narrow limits on the ability of members to pursue different monetary and credit policies and it demands a high degree of *de facto* policy harmonisation. This does not, of course, imply that each country has to experience the same rates of growth of national income, of credit expansion or of prices. Individual country growth rates of real income will be determined largely by domestic conditions of supply and by capital inflows.

Any attempt to evaluate the impact of the Monetary Union on the economic performance of its members is bound to be beset by difficulties. Differences certainly exist between the performance of the member countries of the Monetary Union and the average performance of other African countries not forming part of a monetary union, with respect to a variety of indicators – growth rates, savings rates, inflation rates, and so on, but it would be rash to attribute such differences exclusively, or even mainly, to membership of the Monetary Union. Indeed the differences amongst the members of the Monetary Union are in these respects as great, if not greater, than those between the Union and other countries. Nevertheless, there is certainly no evidence that membership of the Union has been disadvantageous, and in certain respects – that is, in their lower rates of inflation at the end of the decade – observed differences appear to favour the Union. Although membership of the Monetary Union does imply constraints on the use of interest rate and exchange rate policies, because of the difficulty of getting agreement of all members on changes, it does not appear that African countries that are not members of monetary unions have followed any more active interest rate or exchange rate policies than the members of the Union. To that extent it might reasonably be concluded that any macroeconomic costs that might have to be offset against the trade, investment and reserve economisation advantages of monetary union can tentatively be discounted.

Much broader comparative studies also point in the same direction. For instance, during the past decade, countries undertaking IMF-supported policy adjustments to restore equilibrium in their balance of payments recorded significant reductions in their external deficits, but they exhibited only marginal changes in their growth rates of real GDP and consumption. The latter changes, moreover, were not significantly different from those experienced by non-oil developing countries in general (Donovan, 1982, p. 197). These results might also – with due caution – be taken to suggest that the macroeconomic costs of pursuing the monetary and fiscal policies that are a precondition of monetary integration need not be damaging for developing countries.

THE WEST AFRICAN CLEARING HOUSE (WACH)

In the first part of this chapter it was noted that it might be possible to secure certain subsidiary benefits of monetary integration in a trade grouping lacking a common currency, by means of devices such as credit agreements, payments arrangements, and arrangements for reserve pooling. For practical purposes, ECOWAS is now served (excepting only Cape Verde) by an institutionalised payments arrangement, the West African Clearing House (WACH). The Clearing House was established in 1975 in Freetown and commenced operations in 1976.

The role of the Clearing House must be seen against the background of the established modes of settlement for intra-regional transactions. With the exception of unrecorded and recorded border trade, which is normally transacted in cash, often through a parallel market utilising a convertible currency such as the CFA franc, the principal channel for effecting settlements is through the region's commercial banks. They in turn settle in convertible currencies through correspondent banks in the major financial centres of Western Europe (London and Paris) and the United States.

This was the system that the establishment of the Clearing House was designed to improve upon. According to Article 2 of its Articles of Agreement, its objectives are: to promote the use of the currencies of the members of the Clearing House for sub-regional trade and other transactions; to bring about economies in the use of foreign reserves of the members of the Clearing House; to encourage the members of the Clearing House to liberalise trade among their respective countries; and to promote monetary cooperation and consultation among members of the Clearing House.

Since the inception of the Clearing House, Guinea, Guinea–Bissau and Mauretania have joined the original founding members, so that Cape Verde is the sole member of ECOWAS that is not also a participant in the Clearing House. With these accessions, the governing body of the Clearing House (the Exchange and Clearing Committee – EEC), together with its *alter ego* the Committee of West African Central Banks, constitute an institution that can perform for ECOWAS the functions envisaged in Article 38 of the Treaty of overseeing payments and making recommendations on clearing and monetary issues to the Council of Ministers of the Community.

WACH is essentially a centralised clearing system in which transactions invoiced in the local currency of the country of origin are expressed in the unit of account of the centralised clearing system for debit and credit entries to be made against each member central bank. Entries do not give rise to payments until pre-arranged dates, when credits are multilaterally offset against debits, leaving only the outstanding balances to be settled. The system thus reduces the need, on the part of member banks, to have recourse to foreign exchange to settle day-to-day transactions, and permits economies in the use of foreign exchange reserves. The arrangement is not designed to provide credit, apart from interim finance between settlement dates.

The principal tangible benefit to be anticipated from the arrangement is a reduction in the cost of servicing intra-regional trade. Since intra-regional transactions are denominated in a common unit of account, and member banks agree to deal in one another's currency, importers and exporters together should jointly capture the spread between purchase and sale rates of the key international currencies and other foreign-exchange-related charges. A further net gain should accrue to the sub-region as a whole to the extent that commissions paid to foreign banks in the international exchange markets for transfer charges, fees for confirmation of letters of credit and charges on exchange are reduced as a result of this arrangement.

As to its broader objectives, the extent of monetary policy harmonisation required by the clearing arrangement is evidently negligible. Nevertheless, the Clearing House provides an operations-based forum for monetary cooperation and consultation among the member central and commercial banks that may facilitate closer harmonisation in future.

The Procedures of the Clearing House

A primary requisite of a clearing house is a stable unit of account in which the transactions of member banks can be expressed and recorded. The instability of key international currencies has led to the adoption of artificial currency units for such purposes. The unit chosen by the West African Clearing House is the West African Unit of Account (WAUA), which is equivalent in value to one Special Drawing Right (SDR) of the International Monetary Fund. Its use has enabled the WAUA to maintain a relative stability since the inception of the Clearing House.

The choice of the WAUA as the unit of account necessitates the daily establishment of the rate of exchange of the currency of each member bank in terms of the WAUA. This rate is the product of the central rate of each currency (that is, the middle of a member bank's buying and selling rates) in terms of its intervention currency and the intervention currency's own rate in terms of the SDR. These daily rates are calculated by the WACH for all member currencies except those that are already linked to the SDR, such as the Sierra Leone leone and the Guinean syli, for which no calculations are required. The other currencies of the member states are either linked to the US dollar, as in the case of Nigeria, Ghana and Guinea–Bissau, to the franc, as in the case of the BCEAO countries and Mali, or to sterling, as in the case of the Gambian dalasi.

To minimise rate fluctuations and reduce the cost of operations, the daily rates are averaged each month within two rate-determination periods for settlement purposes. The average of the daily rates is then applied as the official rate to all settlements in the following determination period. This practice presents a potential exchange risk, but this has been reduced by a decision effective from 1 May 1980 to apply new official exchange rates immediately to Clearing House transactions where changes are in excess of 2.5 per cent.

In the presence of large numbers of inconvertible currencies, the smooth operation of the clearing system evidently depends on an assurance by the central banks of the member countries that they will convert their own currencies freely into the WAUA in respect of transactions cleared through the Clearing House. Under the Clearing House Agreement, all central banks of member countries have accepted this obligation for eligible transactions. In this very limited sense, the inconvertibility of regional currencies can be said to be overcome.

All current account transactions are, however, in principle eligible, together with such other transactions as may be agreed upon by the ECC. The principal current account exclusions are intra-BCEAO transactions and transactions with non-members. In practice, transactions in respect of oil are not channelled through the Clearing House.

The Clearing House Agreement provides for a settlement of net credit and debit positions at the end of each month. The central banks are notified on a weekly basis of their current net position. A settlement before the normal settlement date at the end of each month takes place if the debtor position of any central bank exceeds its maximum credit level of 10 per cent of its average total value of trade (imports plus exports) with other member countries over the three years preceding the year of calculation. The net credit line on the part of a creditor country is limited to 20 per cent of its total trade similarly calculated. These limits can be exceeded by agreement between the central banks involved in the net debtor/creditor relationship. The cases in which net debit lines have been exceeded have so far been few, and the amounts involved small. Settlement of net balances takes place in one of several specified convertible currencies. With the consent of the creditor bank, a debtor bank can delay the settlement of its debt, in which case interest is payable at a rate determined by the Committee.

The Experience of the Clearing System

Available data on transactions through the Clearing House from the beginning of its operations in 1976 are presented in Table 8.1. The absence of reliable data on intra-Community trade for these periods makes it impossible to establish the share of that trade that is channelled through the Clearing House. There is some indication, however, that certain member countries with highly inconvertible currencies – such as Ghana and Guinea – have channelled an increasing proportion of their payments for intra-regional transactions through the

Table 8.1   *West African Clearing House Operations (in millions of WAUA)*

	1976 2nd half	1977 1st half	1977 2nd half	1978 1st half	1978 2nd half	1981 Year	1982 1st half
1. Transactions channelled through WACH	18.4	27.8	17.4	22.4	29.6	167.7	83.3
2. Line 1 adjusted for financial transfers	10.9	19.0	16.0	19.0	16.7	24.8	25.8
3. Amounts cleared in WACH	4.3	6.8	6.2	7.9	6.3	29.4	
4. Line 3 as percent of line 1	23%	25%	36%	35%	21%	17.5	
5. Line 3 as percent of line 2	39%	36%	39%	41%	37%		

Sources: IMF (1982); WACH (1981); BCEAO (1982b).

Clearing House. On the other hand, the members of BCEAO do not much use the clearing facility. On balance there may have been some slight increase in the proportion of regional payments made through the Clearing House during the past five years.

Table 8.1 also provides an indicator of the reduced requirement for foreign exchange on the part of the central banks in the shape of the amounts cleared (line 3). This amount can be taken to represent settlements of regional transactions that do not necessitate a transfer of foreign exchange in convertible currencies from one central bank to another.

The clearing arrangement was originally justified largely in terms of its providing a framework through which certain deficiencies in the established traditional banking facilities might be minimised. It was expected to eliminate or minimise the delays in settlement that characterised trade transactions among some countries in the sub-region when payments were routed through Europe and the USA. It was also expected to simplify the typically cumbersome settlement procedures for exporters and importers. Experience of the clearing mechanism after five years of operation suggests that the new system has not lived up to expectations and that it has deficiencies that aggravate the payments problems involved in intra-regional financial transactions.

Delays in payments are the most frequently cited problem of the clearing mechanism (IMF, 1982). Final settlements may take as long as four to six months. These delays impose money costs that in practice fall on exporters, which is an important obstacle to intra-regional trade expansion. Delays can occur at any of the three levels of the clearing arrangement: the commercial bank level, the level of national central banks, and the level of the Clearing House itself. Apart from delays that can be laid at the door of the financial institutions, other delays arise because of the inadequate West African regional communications system, which makes direct contacts between members of the Community often less rapid and efficient than contact undertaken indirectly via Europe.

The importance of these criticisms of the clearing system should not be exaggerated. What is relevant is the relative delays that arise under the clearing system by comparison with those that arise when established commercial clearing procedures are followed, which can sometimes be considerable – an unpublished study recently reported that inter-bank transactions in Senegal can take up to a year!

What does seem clear is that the inability of the clearing system to offer an improved service – in part because the approval of national central banks is still required, in part because of a highly complex system at the level of the Clearing House – has led to a continued reliance on the established channels, which, so far, have not been demonstrated to be inferior.

To prevent the stagnation of the clearing system, the Executive Secretary of WACH has proposed (WACH, 1982) that the use of the clearing system should be made obligatory for primary banks, but this proposal was not approved by the Committee, which does not regard the extension of the system as an end in itself.

The idealised picture of the role of the Clearing House that is sometimes drawn (Osagie, 1979) is evidently far from the reality. The Clearing House will only achieve a major role when, in terms of costs and efficiency, its transactions are demonstrably in the interests of the private user as well as of the region's central banks. There is no reason why this objective should not eventually be achieved. Meanwhile, the mechanism itself does little to support economic integration at the clearing level, although the potential importance of the consultative mechanism that it encourages in promoting necessary alignments of monetary policies should not be disregarded.

CONCLUSION

This chapter has reviewed some of the principal issues that arise in connection with monetary aspects of economic integration in West Africa. It has focused particular attention upon those areas of monetary and exchange policy where further harmonisation is required if present trade groupings are to be effective. It has also reviewed the operations of the West African Monetary Union, which embraces six member states of ECOWAS that together account for 15 per cent of the group's GDP and the bulk of its recorded intra-regional trade in manufactured products. The level of that trade has undoubtedly been facilitated by the existence of the convertible currency that the Union affords. Finally the structure and experience of the West African Clearing House has been briefly outlined.

In respect of economic integration in West Africa, the urgent need in monetary affairs is not for monetary integration in a classical sense, but for the *de facto* harmonisation of monetary policy in order to produce a more uniform degree of effective convertibility. So long as the CFA system continues to operate, that must entail more effective convertibility at large.

A decade ago this might have appeared to be an impossible target. But today, with a better understanding of the limitations of expansionary monetary and fiscal policies as development instruments, there is perhaps more reason for hoping that monetary factors need not, in the long run, impede the process of West African economic integration. But the transitional difficulties that confront economic integration from the monetary sphere are immense, and they are unlikely to be easily resolved without a substantial aid inflow to facilitate the adjustment policies that will certainly be a prerequisite.

9 Conclusions

Economic integration in West Africa is clearly not a panacea and it is unlikely alone to generate rapid economic growth. Nevertheless, viewed as a policy alternative to a continued reliance on capital-intensive import-substitution policies directed towards national markets that are in most cases extremely small, it holds out the prospect of important potential benefits. The extent to which those benefits are realised will depend on many factors, but in particular on the ways in which certain key issues – development strategy; the distribution of benefits and the problems of the less developed members; and policy towards foreign direct investment – are resolved. It may be useful in conclusion summarily to compare and contrast some aspects of the four schemes that have been evaluated in this study from these standpoints.

Let us begin with CEAO. In a fundamental sense, a development strategy finds its embodiment in the structure and level of a community's external tariff and in its member states' harmonised investment incentives. In that sense there is as yet no determined development strategy in CEAO – any more than there is in the other groups. But this deficiency, which may yet be overcome, is less damaging for CEAO than it is for ECOWAS because the CEAO system is a coherent one at any stage. It leaves each member state substantial discretion with respect to its degree of market integration with its partners. Each country remains free at present to evaluate economic development issues according to its own criteria and to arrange the modalities of integration accordingly. Integration of product markets and trade liberalisation are underpinned by a scheme that provides compensation for losses from trade diversion arising from trade liberalisation, with a small measure of redistribution through overcompensation. Compensation is not provided for any losses that might arise from trade creation, but this is immaterial since each country can effectively avert the loss of any high-cost industries and also retains policy flexibility with respect to the establishment of new ones. Consequently, even before industrial harmonisation is attained, a country's interests should not be damaged. This is a workable basis for limited cooperation, and it minimises distributional difficulties and harmonisation problems. But a corollary is that the opportunities it affords for generating economic gains are likely to be modest. This is partly bound up with the third issue – namely, policy towards direct foreign investment – where little or no progress is discernible, fundamentally because there is no agreed development strategy, or regional industrial policy or system of investment incentives. At the industrial level, these deficiencies are reflected in the replication of identical plants, which underlines the benefits forgone by failing to promote an optimal pattern of regional industrial specialisation. Industrial harmonisation is urgently needed to maximise integration gains.

Nevertheless, the system is coherent and possesses intrinsic stability. But because it is stable, the danger is that in the absence of strong leadership it merely encourages low sight-setting in the field of integration, and its procedures provide no strong stimulus to further integration.

The Mano River Union is in conception and strategy different. The Union did not attempt – probably wisely – to promote trade liberalisation before agreement had been reached on a common external tariff. The Union's common external tariff does up to a point imply a development strategy – in terms of resource allocation – but since investment incentives are not yet harmonised it represents only a partial approach to this issue. Moreover, there is little evidence that the tariff was constructed in the light of appraisals of Union comparative advantage. To that extent it does not represent a deliberately chosen strategy. Economic disparities between the member states are less wide in the MRU than in the other groups, which may partly explain the absence of compensation provisions in the trade liberalisation aspects of the Union. This could give rise to difficulties if trade liberalisation should be accompanied by a markedly unbalanced pattern of intra-Union trade. But in practice, non-tariff barriers are likely to prevent this from happening. In any case, to the extent that expanded trade is more likely to arise from the Union industry programme, trade imbalance is less likely to be important since the Union industry procedure clearly provides an instrument for developing balanced industrial packages. The construction of such packages should be facilitated by the provision for offsetting any costs of uneconomic location that may be imposed on industries by the need for balanced programmes of Union industries. A common investment code governing incentives that may be offered to foreign investment has not yet been elaborated in the Union but no radical policies appear to be under contemplation.

The issues surrounding ECOWAS are rather different. ECOWAS has been equipped with an elaborate Treaty that left most issues to be resolved subsequently. As an integration strategy this approach has many precedents, though perhaps nowhere else has it been pursued so rigorously. Such an approach, inspired by functionalism, does not of course induce difficulties to disappear, it merely puts off the need to resolve them. It is perhaps to be regretted that having devised a Treaty whose general provisions are coherent and ultimately mutually reinforcing, the Community should nevertheless have decided to follow its implementation procedures to the letter, since these, by giving primacy to market integration and free competition, may well hinder the integration process.

ECOWAS does not yet have a development strategy, except in the limited sense that competition is to be emphasised. There is no external tariff, and no indication in the Treaty as to how it is to be arrived at – unlike the situation with the Treaty of Rome. The Treaty requires that trade liberalisation should take place in advance of tariff harmonisation – unlike the procedure followed in other communities where liberalisation has been made conditional on prior tariff harmonisation, so providing at one and the same time a stimulus to the formation of a common external tariff and avoiding possible misallocations of resources that might otherwise be produced.

But even if the Community's approach is thought reasonable in terms of resource allocation considerations, its attempt to liberalise trade in advance of significant positive measures of integration promises to be counterproductive. Essentially this is because trade liberalisation is likely to benefit mainly the more advanced members, whereas the less advanced members can expect to benefit only from positive integration measures such as overcompensation, from the encouragement of their industrial development through the actions of the ECOWAS Fund, and from appropriate fiscal and industrial harmonisation measures. In itself, the compensation scheme of ECOWAS does virtually nothing to deal with their problems. Awareness of this may induce the less developed members to resist implementation of the liberalisation programme. There are some signs that this may be happening.

A judgement on the merits of the Community's approach must rest largely on strategic considerations. Is it likely that it will help or hinder the process of reaching agreement on measures for positive integration? It is possible that trade liberalisation introduced without concomitant policy measures of fiscal and industrial harmonisation might generate irresistible pressures to move forward, because the alternative would not be – as in CEAO – stability or stagnation at the low level of cooperation that would then have been attained, but, almost certainly, a politically damaging collapse. But this is a high-risk policy. The alternative would be to revamp the stages of integration envisaged – or since this would be very difficult, to promptly introduce built-in safeguards for at least the less developed members during the trade liberalisation phase and prior to the implementation of positive integration measures at the Community level. Given strong leadership, such an alternative approach might provide a better framework within which functionalist integrative forces could constructively operate.

In respect of policies towards foreign direct investment, ECOWAS shows signs of wishing to develop a more positive approach than the other two groups. Certainly bargaining with multinationals appears to have been very much in the minds of those who devised the arrangements. Any useful policy in this field will ultimately have to rest on a harmonisation of investment incentives and of industrial development programmes, since it is basically the lack of such harmonisation that produces the effects or abuses of which developing countries complain, and that may tip the balance of benefits unduly in the favour of the foreign investor. So far the only initiative in this area within ECOWAS is the local participation provision in its rules of origin. In themselves, these provisions are likely to exacerbate the problem of the less developed members and, without a prior harmonisation of investment incentives, they are unlikely to remedy the specific problems aimed at, of which formal ownership is only one aspect.

The central issues of the Senegambian initiative are different again, and in one sense narrower than those discussed already. There are two sets of problems – those that typically arise in any customs union between an industrially more advanced and an industrially less advanced country, and the unique additional problem presented by the magnitude of clandestine trade between the two prospective member countries. If there is to be a full customs union between Senegal and The Gambia, it would not be possible for its prospective disadvantages for The Gambia in the shape of trade diversion to be overcome and for The Gambia to derive positive benefits unless union were to be accompanied by negotiated benefits in relation to one or more of: revenue allocation, industrial development, transport and service development.

It would not be difficult to devise arrangements that could preserve the interests of The Gambia with respect to Senegal in the period before ECOWAS obligations become operative for both parties. But in the longer run, with or without confederation, the existence of ECOWAS obligations would make it difficult if not impossible to guarantee the interests of The Gambia with respect to Senegal, for the provisions of the Treaty of Lagos that are designed to safeguard the interests of the less developed members of the Community *vis-à-vis* industrially more advanced members (and on which The Gambia would have to rely) are of questionable value. The interests of The

Gambia with respect to Senegal and Senegambian confederation will be safeguarded in the context of ECOWAS only if improved safeguards for its less developed members are introduced.

All four West African groupings are prisoners of an approach to integration that can be justified only in terms of functionalist strategic considerations. Immense efforts have been devoted to the reduction of tariff barriers on an across-the-board basis and to the creation of an apparatus of 'holistic' integration that is appropriate if at all only to intimate economic communities. Yet economic integration in West Africa is likely to make a significant contribution to development – and thus establish its claim to survival – only to the extent that it results in a rationalisation of industrial development on an acceptable regional basis. The principal instruments and compromises necessary to make a reality of this task are not yet properly established in any of the groupings. One obstacle is that in no case have the special difficulties of the numerically dominant less developed members been adequately recognised. A further obstacle is that the overwhelmingly important non-tariff aspects of cooperation have been assigned a second place – including monetary cooperation and convertibility – and their lack is probably a more important obstacle to trade expansion than are tariff barriers.

It would be presumptuous to condemn this strategy – the political dynamics of regional integration are complex and uncertain. However persuasive a more limited approach to integration founded on selective industrial cooperation might be (Vaitsos, 1980; Robson, 1980), there can obviously be no assurance that it would in the end be any more productive. But it can hardly be questioned that regional groupings whose common institutions lack a strong capacity to identity, evaluate and promote significant industrial (and infrastructural) cooperation projects and to identify concrete development gains for its members will find it difficult if not impossible to develop the impetus needed to sustain fruitful regional cooperation. To develop a West African capacity in these fields, greatly strengthened Community Funds and development banking institutions would be necessary. At a national level, priority needs to be given to those specific adjustments that would be required to implement joint projects. A willingness to develop effective instruments for industrial cooperation, and to use them, is likely to be the single most crucial determinant of the future role of regional integration in West Africa – and, no doubt, of similar arrangements in other less developed regions.

Bibliography

Adedeji, Adebayo (1976), 'Collective self-reliance in developing Africa: scope, prospects and problems', Keynote address at the International Conference on the Economic Community of West African States (Lagos: Nigerian Institute of International Affairs).

Africa Research (1964–), *Africa Research Bulletin* (Exeter: Africa Research Ltd, monthly).

African Centre for Monetary Studies (1979), *Balance of Payments Problems of African Countries and their Effects on Development Objectives* (Dakar: African Centre for Monetary Studies).

African Centre for Monetary Studies (1981), 'Monetary theory and policy in Africa', mimeo (Dakar: African Centre for Monetary Studies).

Allen, P. (1976), *Organisation and Administration of a Monetary Union*, Essays in International Finance, no. 38 (Princeton, NJ: International Finance Section, Princeton University).

Aschheim, J. and Park, Y. S. (1976), *Artificial Currency Units: The Formation of Functional Currency Areas*, Essays in International Finance, no. 114 (Princeton, NJ: International Finance Section, Princeton University).

Balassa, B. (1978), 'Avantages comparés et perspectives de l'intégration économique en Afrique de l'Ouest', in *Colloque sur l'integration en Afrique de l'Ouest* (Dakar: Université de Dakar, Faculté des Sciences Juridiques et Economiques).

Balassa, B. (1982), *Development Strategies in Semi-Industrialised Economies* (Baltimore, Md.: The Johns Hopkins University Press).

Banque Centrale des Etats de l'Afrique de l'Ouest, *Notes d'Information et Statistiques* (Dakar: BCEAO, monthly).

Banque Centrale des Etats de l'Afrique de l'Ouest (1982a), *Rapport d'activité 1981* (Dakar: BCEAO).

Banque Centrale des Etats de l'Afrique de l'Ouest (1982b), *Note d'information*, no. 307 (July 1982). Report of the 12th Annual meeting of the Committee of West African Central Banks, and the 7th meeting of the Exchange and Compensation Committee of the WACH.

Banque Ouest-Africaine de Développement (1978), *La Coopération régionale et le financement des investissements dans l'Union Monétaire Ouest-Africaine* (Lomé: BOAD).

Behrman, J. (1972), *The Role of International Companies in Latin American Integration* (Lexington, Mass: Lexington Books).

Bhatia, R. J. (1982), *The West African Monetary Union – Experience in Monetary Arrangements, 1963–74* (Washington, DC: International Monetary Fund).

Black, S. W. (1976), *Exchange Policies for Less Developed Countries in a World of Floating Rates*, Essays in International Finance, no. 119 (Princeton, NJ: International Finance Section, Princeton University).

Bridges, R. C. (ed.) (1974), *Senegambia: Proceedings of a Colloquium at the University of Aberdeen* (Aberdeen: Aberdeen University African Studies Group).

Byé, M. (1950), 'Unions douanières et données nationales', *Economie Appliquée*, vol. 3, pp. 121–57. Reprinted in translation as 'Customs unions and national interests', *International Economic Papers*, no. 3, 1953.

Carnoy, M. (1972), *Industrialization in a Latin American Common Market* (Washington, DC: The Brookings Institution).

Clapham, Christopher (1976), *Liberia and Sierra Leone: An Essay in Comparative Politics* (Cambridge: Cambridge University Press).

Commonwealth Secretariat (1978), *The Mano River Union: An Assessment of Past Performance and Some Guidelines for the Future* (London: Commonwealth Secretariat).

Commonwealth Secretariat (1979), *Report on the Harmonisation of Fiscal Incentives to Industry in the Mano River Union* (London: Commonwealth Secretariat).

Communauté Economique de l'Afrique de l'Ouest (1974–), *Journal Officiel* (Ouagadougou: CEAO).

Communauté Economique de l'Afrique de l'Ouest (1978–), *Intégration africaine: Revue trimestrielle de la CEAO* (Ouagadougou: CEAO).

Communauté Economique de l'Afrique de l'Ouest (1973), *Traité et protocoles instituant la C.E.A.O.* (Abidjan: CEAO).

Communauté Economique de l'Afrique de l'Ouest (1977), *Rapport d'activités: Année 1976* (Ouagadougou: CEAO).

Communauté Economique de l'Afrique de l'Ouest (1978), *Rapport d'activités – 1977–78* (Ouagadougou: CEAO).

Communauté Economique de l'Afrique de l'Ouest (1979a), *Note de synthèse du rapport d'activités 1978/79* (Ouagadougou: CEAO).

Communauté Economique de l'Afrique de l'Ouest (1979b), *Tarif d'usage T.C.R.* (Ouagadougou: CEAO).

Communauté Economique de l'Afrique de l'Ouest (1979c), *Statistiques des produits agrées à la T.C.R. 1976–1977–1978* (Ouagadougou: CEAO).

Communauté Economique de l'Afrique de l'Ouest (1980), *Fonds Communautaire de Développement: Prévisions de recettes 1980.2è version* (Ouagadougou: CEAO).

Cooper, C. A. and Massell, B. F. (1965), 'Towards a general theory of customs unions for developing countries', *Journal of Political Economy*, vol. 73, pp. 461–76.

Cooper, R. N. (1969), 'Discussion', in R. A. Mundell and A. K. Swoboda (eds), *Monetary Problems of the International Economy* (Chicago, Ill.: Chicago University Press), pp. 164–5.

Corden, W. M. (1971), 'The effects of trade on the rate of growth', in J. Bhagwati *et al.* (eds), *Trade, Balance of Payments and Growth* (Amsterdam: North Holland), pp. 117–43.

Corden, W. M. (1972), 'Economies of scale and customs union theory', *Journal of Political Economy*, vol. 80, pp. 465–75.

Corden, W. M. (1974), *Trade Policy and Economic Welfare* (Oxford: Clarendon Press).

Dervis, K. *et al.* (1982), *General Equilibrium Models for Development Policy* (London: Cambridge University Press).

Donovan, D. J. (1982), 'Macroeconomic performance and adjustment under

Fund-supplied programmes; the experience of the seventies', *International Monetary Fund Staff Papers*, vol. 29, pp. 171–203.

Dosser, D. (1972), 'Customs unions, tax unions and development unions', in R. M. Bird and J. G. Head (eds), *Modern Fiscal Issues: Essays in Honor of Carl S. Shoup* (Toronto: Toronto University Press), pp. 86–103.

Dunn, John (ed.) (1978), *West African States: Failure and Promise* (Cambridge: Cambridge University Press).

Dunning, J. H. (1981), *International Production and the Multinational Enterprise* (London: Allen & Unwin).

Economic Community of West African States (1976a), *Treaty of the Economic Community of West African States* (Lagos: ECOWAS).

Economic Community of West African States (1976b), *Protocols Annexed to the Treaty of ECOWAS* (Lagos: ECOWAS).

Economic Community of West African States (1979–), *Official Journal: Protocols, Decisions and Directives* (Lagos: ECOWAS).

Findlay, R. (1971), 'Comparative advantage, effective protection and the domestic resource cost of foreign exchange', *Journal of International Economics*, vol. 1, pp. 189–204.

Fonds de Solidarité et d'Intervention pour le Développement de la Communauté Economique de l'Afrique de l'Ouest (1980), *Rapport final de la 2ᵉ session du conseil d'administration* (Ouagadougou: FOSIDEC).

Gambia (1964), *Report on the Alternatives for Association between The Gambia and Senegal*, Sessional Paper no. 13 of 1964 (Bathurst: Government Printer).

Gambia (1981a), *Five-Year Development Plan 1981–2 – 1985–6* (Banjul: Government Printer).

Gambia (1981b), 'The Confederation Agreement', *Gambia News Bulletin*, no. 141, 30 December (Banjul: Ministry of Information).

Guillaumont, P. and S. (1981), *Problèmes posés par le régime des changes des pays africains ayant pour monnaie les francs CFA* (Clermont: Centre d'Etudes et de Recherches sur le Développement International).

Hazlewood, A. (1975), *Economic Integration: The East African Experience* (London: Heinemann Educational Books).

Horst, T. (1973), 'The simple analytics of multi-national firm behaviour', in M. B. Connolly and A. K. Swoboda (eds), *International Trade and Money* (London: Allen & Unwin), pp. 72–84.

Hughes, Arnold (1974), 'Senegambia revisited: or changing Gambian perceptions of integration with Senegal', in *Senegambia: Proceedings of a Colloquium at the University of Aberdeen* (Aberdeen: Aberdeen University African Studies Group), pp. 139–70.

International Monetary Fund (1982), *Currency Convertibility in the Economic Community of West African States* (Washington, DC: IMF).

Ishiyama, Y. (1975), 'The theory of optimum currency areas: a survey', *International Monetary Fund Staff Papers*, vol. 22, pp. 344–83.

Johnson, H. G. (1970), 'The efficiency and welfare implications of the international corporation', in C. P. Kindleberger (ed.), *The International Corporation* (Cambridge, Mass.: MIT Press), pp. 35–56.

Kafka, A. (1969), 'Regional monetary integration of the developing countries', in R. A. Mundell and A. K. Swoboda (eds), *Monetary Problems of the International Economy* (Chicago, Ill.: Chicago University Press), pp. 135–43.

Kemp, M. C. (1969), *A Contribution to the General Equilibrium Theory of Preferential Trading* (Amsterdam: North Holland).

Kirkpatrick, C. and Nixson, F. (1981), 'Transnational corporations and development', *Journal of Modern African Studies*, vol. 19, pp. 367–99.

Krueger, A. (1969), 'Discussion', in R. A. Mundell and A. K. Swoboda (eds), *Monetary Problems of the International Economy* (Chicago, Ill.: Chicago University Press), p. 169.

Kuyvenhoven, A. and Mennes, L. B. M. (1980), 'Les projets de coopération régionale: identification, selection, évaluation et implantation', *Industrie et Développement*, no. 1 (1980), pp. 3–41.

Langdon, S. and Mytelka, L. K. (1979), 'Africa in the changing world economy', in C. Legum *et al.*, *Africa in the 1980s* (New York, NY: McGraw-Hill).

Leite, S. P. (1982), 'Interest rate policies in West Africa', *International Monetary Fund Staff Papers*, vol. 29, pp. 48–76.

Lent, G. E. (1974), *Harmonisation of Investment Incentives for Liberia–Sierra Leone's Joint Economic Development* (Monrovia: Revenue Symposium).

Liberia (1977), *Economic Survey* (Monrovia: Ministry of Economic Planning).

Lipschitz, L. (1979), 'Exchange rate policy for a small developing country, and the selection of an appropriate standard', *International Monetary Fund Staff Papers*, vol. 26, pp. 423–49.

Little, I. M. D. and Mirrlees, J. (1974), *Project Appraisal and Planning for Developing Countries* (London: Heinemann Educational Books).

MacDougall, G. D. A. (1960), 'The benefits and costs of private investment from abroad: a theoretical approach', *Economic Record*, vol. 36, pp. 13–35.

Mano River Union (1976a), *Appraisal of the Proposals for a Union (Harmonised) – External Tariff Schedule* (Freetown: MRU).

Mano River Union (1976b), *The Mano River Declaration* (Freetown: MRU).

Mano River Union (1977), *Common External Tariff* (Freetown: MRU).

Mano River Union (1978a), *Minutes, Union Commission on Industry and Trade, Third Meeting* (Freetown: MRU).

Mano River Union (1978b), *Report, Union Ministerial Council, Fifth Ordinary Session, Monrovia* (Freetown: MRU).

Mano River Union (1978c), *Annual Report 1977–78* (Freetown: MRU).

Mano River Union (1979), *The Mano River Declaration and Protocols* (Freetown: MRU).

Mano River Union (1980a), *Regulations for the Administration of Trade in Goods of Local Origin Between the Member-States of the Mano River Union* (Freetown: MRU).

Mano River Union (1980b), *Intra-Union Trade* (Freetown: MRU).

Mano River Union (1981), *Annual Report, 1980–81* (Freetown: MRU).

Mennes, L. B. M. (1973), *Planning and Economic Integration Among Developing Countries* (Rotterdam: University Press).

Monson, T. D. (1974), 'The evolution of West African trade during the 1960s: implications for regional economic integration', mimeo. (Abidjan: CIRES).

Mswaka, T. (1974), 'Tariff structure and economic cooperation between Liberia and Sierra Leone', *The Economic Bulletin of Ghana*, vol. 4, pp. 33–51.

Mytelka, L. (1979) *Regional Development in a Global Economy* (New Haven, Conn. and London: Yale University Press).

Nana-Sinkam, S. C. (1978), *Monetary Integration and the Theory of Optimum Currency Areas in Africa* (The Hague: Mouton).

Ojo, O. J. B. (1980), 'Nigeria and the formation of ECOWAS', *International Organisation*, vol. 34, no. 4, pp. 571–604.

Ojo, O. J. B. (1981), 'Oil, politics and core-state integration policy: Nigeria and ECOWAS', Manuscript.

Onitiri, H. M. (1963), 'Towards a West African economic community', *Nigerian Journal of Economic and Social Studies*, vol. 5, pp. 15–26.

Osagie, E. (1979), 'West African Clearing House, West African Unit of Account, and pressures for monetary integration', *Journal of Common Market Studies*, vol. 17, pp. 227–35.

Pearson, S. R. and Ingram, W. D. (1980), 'Economies of scale, domestic divergences, and potential gains from economic integration in Ghana and the Ivory Coast', *Journal of Political Economy*, vol. 88, pp. 994–1008.

Robson, P. (1968), *Economic Integration in Africa* (London: Allen & Unwin).

Robson, P. (1971), *Fiscal Compensation and the Distribution of Benefits in Economic Groupings of Developing Countries* (New York: United Nations).

Robson, P. (ed.) (1972), *International Economic Integration* (London: Penguin Books).

Robson, P. (1980), *The Economics of International Integration* (London: Allen & Unwin).

Robson, P. (1981), 'Regional economic cooperation among developing countries: some further considerations', in P. Streeten and R. Jolly (eds), *Recent Issues in Word Development* (Oxford: Pergamon), pp. 331–7.

Scully, G. W. and Yu, E. S. H. (1974), 'International investment, trade diversion and trade creation', *Economic Record*, vol. 50, pp. 600–4.

Senegalo-Gambian Permanent Secretariat (1976), *Senegalo-Gambian Agreements* (Banjul: Senegalo-Gambian Permanent Secretariat).

Sesay, Amadu (1980), 'Conflict and collaboration: Sierra Leone and her West African neighbours, 1961–80', *Afrika Spectrum*, no. 2, pp. 163–80.

Sierra Leone (1974), *Development Plan 1974–5 – 1978–9* (Freetown: Government Printer).

Sierra Leone (1977), *Annual Plan, 1977–78* (Freetown: Government Printer).

Tarr, B. (1974), 'Towards harmonising customs and excise taxes between Liberia and Sierra Leone', mimeo. (Monrovia: Revenue Symposium).

Taylor, A. B. (1974), 'Revenue effects on Liberia and Sierra Leone of mutual removal of tariff and non-tariff barriers', mimeo. (Monrovia: Revenue Symposium)

Thompson, V. (1972), *West Africa's Consiel de l'Entente* (Ithaca, NY: Cornell University Press).

Thompson, V. and Adloff, R. (1958), *French West Africa* (London: Allen & Unwin).

Tinbergen, J. (1965), *International Economic Integration*, 2nd edn (Amsterdam: Elsevier).

Tironi, E. (1982), 'Customs unions theory in the presence of foreign firms', *Oxford Economic Papers*, vol. 34, pp. 150–71.

United Nations Conference on Trade and Development (1973), *Report of the United Nations Interdisciplinary Mission to Review the Scope for Inter-Regional and International Cooperation between Sierra Leone and Liberia* (Geneva: UNCTAD).

United Nations Conference on Trade and Development (1978), *Transnational Corporations and Expansion of Trade in Manufactures and Semi-Manufactures* (Geneva: UNCTAD).

United Nations Conference on Trade and Development (1979), *Monetary and Financial Obstacles to Trade Expansion and Possible Improvements in Payments Relations* [in Economic Community of West African States] (Geneva: UNCTAD).

United Nations Conference on Trade and Development (1980), *Handbook of International Trade and Development Statistics: Supplement* (Geneva: UNCTAD).

United Nations Conference on Trade and Development (1981), *Trade Among Developing Countries by Main SITC Groups and by Regions* (Geneva: UNCTAD).

United Nations Economic Commission for Africa (1978), *Study of Recorded Trade Flows* [of Economic Community of West African States] (Addis Ababa: ECA).

United Nations Economic Commission for Africa (1979), *Unrecorded Trade Flows Within ECOWAS* (Addis Ababa: ECA).

United Nations Economic Commission for Africa (1981), *Report of the ECA Mission on the Evaluation of UDEAC* (Libreville: Gabon).

United Nations Economic Commission for Asia and the Far East (1973), *Asian Industrial Survey for Regional Co-Operation* (New York, NY: United Nations).

United Nations Industrial Development Organisation (1970), *Final Report to the Government of The Gambia by the Industrial Survey Mission of the UNIDO* (Vienna: UNIDO).

United Nations Industrial Development Organisation (1976), *Mano River Union Industry Studies* (Vienna: UNIDO).

Vaitsos, C. (1974), 'Income distribution and welfare considerations', in J. H. Dunning (ed.), *Economic Analysis and the Multinational Enterprise* (London: Allen & Unwin), pp. 300–41.

Vaitsos, C. (1978a), 'The attitudes and role of transnational enterprises in economic integration processes among the LDCs', *Millenium: Journal of International Studies*, vol. 6, pp. 251–69.

Vaitsos, C. (1978b), 'The crisis in economic co-operation among developing countries', *World Development*, vol. 6, pp. 719–69. Reprinted in P. Streeten and R. Jolly (eds), *Recent Issues in World Development* (Oxford: Pergamon, 1981).

Vaitsos, C. (1980), 'Corporate integration in world production and trade', in D. Seers and C. Vaitsos (eds), *Integration and Unequal Development* (London: Macmillan), pp. 24–45.

Viner, J. (1950), *The Customs Union Issue* (New York, NY: Carnegie Endowment for International Peace; London: Stevens & Sons).

Voss, Harald (1979), 'Kooperation in West Afrika: multilaterale institutionen und bilaterale zusammenarbeit', *Afrika Spectrum*, no 2, pp. 151–76.

West African Clearing House (1981), *Annual Report 1980–1981* (Freetown: WACH).

West African Clearing House (1982), *Report of the 7th Ordinary Meeting of the EEC of the WACH, Note d'Information*, no. 307 (Dakar: Banque Centrale des Etats de l'Afrique de l'Ouest).

Westphal, L. E. (1971), *Planning Investments with Economies of Scale* (Amsterdam: North Holland).

Wiles, P. J. D. (1968), *Communist International Economics* (Oxford: Basil Blackwell).

Wonnacott, P. and R. (1981), 'Is unilateral tariff reduction preferable to a customs union? The curious case of the missing foreign tariffs', *American Economic Review*, vol. 71, pp. 704–14.

World Bank (1975), 'Incentives and resource costs in the Ivory Coast', mimeo. (Washington, DC: The World Bank).

World Bank (1976), 'Incentives and comparative advantage in Ghanaian industry and agriculture', mimeo. (Washington, DC: The World Bank).

World Bank (1977a), 'Incentives and comparative advantage in agriculture and industry: Mali', mimeo. (Washington, DC: The World Bank).

World Bank (1977b), 'Incentives and resource costs in Senegal', mimeo. (Washington, DC: The World Bank).

World Bank (1978), *Ivory Coast: The Challenge of Success* (Baltimore, Md.: The Johns Hopkins University Press).

World Bank (1981a), *The Gambia: Basic Needs in The Gambia* (Washington, DC: The World Bank).

World Bank (1981b), *Accelerated Development in Sub-Saharan Africa* (Washington, DC: The World Bank).

World Bank (1982a), *1981 World Bank Atlas* (Washington, DC: The World Bank).

World Bank (1982b), *World Development Report, 1982* (New York, NY: Oxford University Press).

Index

For Product Safety Concerns and Information please contact our EU
representative GPSR@taylorandfrancis.com Taylor & Francis Verlag GmbH,
Kaufingerstraße 24, 80331 München, Germany

Printed and bound by CPI Group (UK) Ltd, Croydon, CR0 4YY
01/05/2025
01858431-0001